IELTS ACADEMIC VOCABULARY

Master 3000+ Academic Vocabularies By Topics Explained In 10 Minutes A Day

RACHEL MITCHELL

ISBN: 9781983305238

TEXT COPYRIGHT © 2018 [RACHEL MITCHELL]

TABLE OF CONTENT

INTRODUCTION

Thank you and congratulate you for downloading the book *"IELTS Academic Vocabulary: Master 3000+ Academic Vocabularies by Topics Explained in 10 Minutes a Day (3 books in 1 Box set)"*

This book is well designed and written by an experienced native teacher from the USA who has been teaching IELTS for over 10 years. She really is the expert in training IELTS for students at each level. In this book, she will provide you with *over 3000 Academic Vocabularies* **explained** to help you easily achieve an **8.0+** for the IELTS *Lexical Resource Band Score*, even if your vocabulary is not rich enough from the beginning. This book will also walk you through all topics, such as *education, work, health, hobbies, the media, books and films, urbanization, environment, weather, climate change and pollution, accommodation, houses, time, travel, tourism & holidays, music, food, technology, friends, towns and cities, family, people and relationships, law, crime and punishment, business, money, shopping, clothes and fashion, etc*; clearly analyze, explain with examples for every single academic word. If you'd like to increase your wide range of IELTS Academic Vocabulary, then this book may be **the most important book** that you will ever read.

As the author of this book, Rachel Mitchell believes that this book will be **an indispensable reference** and **trusted guide** for you who may want to maximize your band score in the IELTS exam. Once you read this book, I guarantee you that you will have learned an extraordinarily wide range of useful, and practical IELTS Academic Words that will help you become a successful IELTS taker as well as you will even become a successful English user in work and in life within a short period of time only.

Take action today and start getting 8.0 + in IELTS tomorrow!

Thank you again for purchasing this book, and I hope you enjoy it.

EDUCATION/ STUDENT'S LIFE

Scholarship *[Noun] (an award of financial support for a student to pursue their higher education).*

He won a scholarship at the age of 16 and was teaching physics at 19.

She won a scholarship to study law at Harvard University.

Admission *[Noun] (the act of accepting or allowing someone to enter a place or organization).*

Many students qualify for admission to the university this year.

He submitted an application for admission to the university.

She applied for admission to the club.

Grant *[Verb] (an amount of money is given to be used for a particular purpose such as education research).*

The college awarded him a grant of $50,000 to study law at Harvard University.

He was granted money to buy a house.

Learning environment *[Noun] (the whole range of conditions and activities in which learning happens).*

The trust and bond between a teacher and students create a perfect learning environment.

My school is the perfect learning environment.

Study abroad *[Verb] (the act of going to a foreign country to study).*

I am going to study abroad next year, but I don't know where.

Study abroad nowadays is one of the fastest ways to enter and settle in your favorite countries.

Gap year *[Noun] (a year between leaving high school and starting university that someone spends on working or travelling).*

Some students decide to take a gap year before they begin university.

After finishing school, she took a gap year and travelled through the UK and Canada.

Gossip *[Verb] (to have a casual conversation).*

She's always gossiping.

I like having a good gossip now and then.

Bookworm *[Noun] (someone who spends a lot of time reading).*

My brother is a bookworm. He is always reading.

I am not a bookworm. I do not like to read.

Distance learning *[Noun] (a system of education in which teachers and students do not meet in a classroom but use the Internet or TV programmes and e-mail to have classes).*

It is possible for pupils in rural communities to take advantage of distance learning educational programmes.

Thanks to distance learning, many students no longer have to attend classes in person, but can study online.

Enroll in *[Verb] (to register, or enter in a list for an activity or for membership in a group).*

Mary has enrolled in an advanced painting class last week in order to improve her craft.

There are currently over 500 students enrolled in our French Language Program.

To play truant = to skive off *[Verb] (to purposefully not attend a class without permission).*

It is bad news when youngsters begin to play truant from school.

He often played truant and wrote his own sick notes.

Absent *[Adjective] (not present in a place where you are expected to be).*

He is often absent from school.

She has been absent from his desk for two weeks.

Do an exam = sit an exam = take an exam *[Verb] (to do a test).*

I have to sit an exam next week.

I'm taking my English exam tomorrow.

To retake a course *[Verb] (to do a course again because you have failed it the first time).*

Students do not need special permission to retake a course.

May I retake a course for a higher grade?

Enforcement *[Noun] (the act of compelling people obey a particular law or rule).*

He works in law enforcement.

The enforcement of laws relating to environmental protection has always been difficult.

At a slow /leisurely pace *[Expression] (at an unhurried, relaxed, slow speed).*

Let's start at a slow pace.

We could walk the entire distance at a slow pace.

We strolled along at a leisurely pace.

A formal examination *[Noun] (a test conducted under strict, regulated conditions).*

She had to take a formal examination before she could graduate.

He is preparing for her certification examination.

To drop out of college *[Verb]* *(to leave college or university before you have finished your studies).*

Too many students drop out of college after only one year.

He dropped out of college after his first semester because of money.

She dropped out of college in her second year.

Preschooler *[Noun]* *(a child not yet old enough to go to school).*

I wanted to see how far my son's concepts went in math when he was a preschooler.

When I was a preschooler, I had a dentist named Dr. Williams.

Vocational school *[Noun]* *(a school which provides students with the special skills and education that they need to do a particular job).*

The curriculum at a vocational school is more career-focused.

The vocational school provides education for young people so that they can qualify themselves.

Productive *[Adjective]* *(producing or achieving a lot of results).*

I had a very productive day of working yesterday.

Our last meeting was very productive.

Primary school *[Noun]* *(a school for children between the ages of five and eleven).*

Learning to write is one of the most important things that a child at primary school will learn.

My sister is a primary school teacher.

I have studied English since I was in a primary school.

Secondary school *[Noun]* *(a school for children who are aged from 11, 16 to 18).*

She taught history at a secondary school.

When I was in a secondary school, all I ever wanted is a job to pay all the bills.

Postgraduate school *[Noun] (a school that awards advanced academic degrees).*

He finally earned a Master degree in post-graduate school.

She is a full-time student on post-graduate school.

Attentive *[Adjective] (paying close attention to something).*

He is an attentive student.

Mary asked Tom to be attentive during meetings.

The speaker likes to have an attentive audience.

To master a language *[Verb] (to learn or understand a language completely).*

If you want to master a language, you need to learn to think in that language.

In order to master a language, you must Listen, Read, Speak, Write, in that order.

Linguistic ability *[Noun] (the ability to master other languages).*

Her linguistic ability served her well in her chosen profession.

The new recruit was tested to have good linguistic ability.

To speak fluently *[Verb] (to speak easily and quickly).*

The students were trained to speak fluently and without unnecessary hesitations.

She speaks several languages fluently.

To take up a language *[Verb] (to start to study a language).*

I've decided to take up a language.

It's just as important to take up a language you enjoy since it would be helpful in everyday life.

Transmission of knowledge *[Noun] (the process of passing knowledge from one person to another).*

Universities are involved in the production and transmission of knowledge.

It's a cultural transmission of knowledge from generation to generation.

Intensive *[Adjective] (involving a lot of work, effort or activity done in a short period of time).*

An intensive course of treatment will take at least several days.

This is an intensive course in business writing.

To pay attention to *[Verb] (to think about, work on, watch, or listen to someone or something carefully).*

He didn't pay attention to details.

She's never paid that much attention to his opinions.

He paid no attention to her warning.

Focus on *[Verb] (to put a lot of your attention on one thing).*

He focused on his studies.

She focused on her work.

Background *[Noun] (the details of a person's family, education, career, wealth).*

Poverty can affect anyone, regardless of age, race, gender or social background.

Despite their different social backgrounds, they became good friends.

Progress rapidly *[Verb] (to grow, improve or develop very quickly).*

Many children who make a slow start but then make progress rapidly.

Julia progresses rapidly in her music lessons.

Adapt *[Verb] (to change something so that it is suitable for a new use or purpose, or in a new situation).*

Tom soon adapted himself to school life.

The young adapted themselves to the change quickly.

Interactive *[Adjective] ((of two or more people or things) acting with each other).*

The class was very interactive during the class discussion.

The training was very interactive.

Her classes were very interactive; students were reading, writing, talking, and reflecting in meaningful ways.

Face-to-face learning *[Noun] (to study in the traditional way, with the teacher and students present in the room).*

In his opinion, face to face learning will benefit the learner the most.

They preferred face-to-face learning for communication purposes.

Learning activities still take place in a face-to-face learning scenario.

To give feedback *[Verb] (to give comments (how well or badly), corrections or information about a person's performance of a task).*

I liked the way the professor gave feedbacks to his students.

Once he found a mistake on the unfinished release draft, he gave feedbacks and corrections immediately.

Interactive learning *[Noun] (refers to a method of teaching and learning in which teachers encourage students to be part of the lesson instead of passive observers (teachers and students acting with each other)).*

Interactive learning is a hands-on approach to help students become more engaged and retain more material.

Each class has been designed to maximise interactive learning, deliberation, and reflection.

Higher education *[Noun] (education beyond high school, usually provided by a college or university).*

Some school leavers prefer to start work rather than enter higher education.

My brother moved to the United Kingdom (UK) to continue his higher education.

A vocational course *[Noun] (a course which provides students with the skills and education that they need to do a particular job).*

For every four students who start a vocational course in upper secondary, one drops out.

Peter chose a vocational course at the secondary level.

To disrupt lessons *[Verb] (to interrupt the lesson by causing a disturbance or problem).*

There are many reasons why pupils disrupt lessons.

It's very hard to call out pupils who consistently talk or disrupt lessons if you don't know their names.

Mandatory *[Adjective] (required, compulsory).*

It is mandatory that all students take two years of English.

It is mandatory to comply with the legislation.

Educational *[Adjective] (relating to education).*

I found our trip very educational.

Watching television can be very educational.

Science programs are very educational and interesting for both children and adults.

Academic *[Adjective] (relating to education, schools, universities, and scholarship).*

These phrases are more suitable for academic essays.

He's certainly bright, but he's not very academic.

Learning atmosphere *[Noun] (the mood or feeling that exists in a class and affects the students who are there).*

Games offer students a fun-filled and relaxing learning atmosphere.

New emerging technology makes learning atmosphere pleasant and conductive.

Extra-curricular activities *[Noun] (not falling within the scope of a regular course, work or studies in school or college).*

The students took a lot of interest in extra-curricular activities.

We have extra-curricular activities after school.

Lecturer *[Noun] (a person who gives lectures at a college or university).*

The lecturer illustrated his point with a diagram on the blackboard.

The lecturer would end up her speech with a joke.

Academic subject *[Noun] (subjects relating to education, schools, universities, etc).*

History is an academic subject.

We've learnt a variety of academic subjects.

Do badly in an exam *[Verb] (if you do badly in an exam it is because the test was too hard).*

She is a good student. She's never done badly in an exam.

Have you ever done badly in an exam?

Transcript *[Noun] (a detailed record of student's marks or grades that they have received at a school).*

If the student wants a copy of his transcript, he should go to the Registrar's Office.

Each applicant must submit his transcript with his application.

Internship *[Noun] (a temporary job that a student or new graduate takes in order to get practical experience in the area they want to work in).*

Your ability to write about your internship experience on your resume is incredibly important.

Jane has a summer internship at a local TV station.

Extracurricular activities *[Noun] (activities that students do at school or college that are not part of their course).*

We have extracurricular activities after school.

Generally, volunteer activities aren't always extracurricular activities.

Social and cultural life *[Noun] (ways of life).*

Advertisements have greatly affected our social and cultural life.

Ethiopia's coffee ceremony is an integral part of their social and cultural life.

Tuition fees *[Noun] (the amount of money that you pay for your education).*

Tuition fees are free and the teaching methods and facilities are great.

The tuition fees went up this year.

Grant *[Verb] (to allow someone to do or have what they want).*

Did they grant Tom permission to leave?

He was granted a patent on his invention.

He was granted admission to the university.

Dormitory *[Noun] (a large room where a lot of people in a school or institution sleep).*

He lived in a college dormitory.

She was reading a math textbook in the dormitory.

He hangs out in the school dormitory.

Reach one's full potential *[Verb] (to take great effort and self-discipline).*

We will help your child reach his full potential.

Our hope for Bill is that he will reach his full potential.

Bachelor's degree *[Noun] (a first university degree (a degree awarded by a college or university)).*

It took him six years to get his bachelor's degree in math.

I graduated from City University with a bachelor's degree in law.

Hit the books *[Verb] (to study very hard).*

I have to go home and hit the books because I have a big test tomorrow.

It's time to hit the books.

Master's degree *[Noun] (an advanced college or university degree, which follows after bachelor's degree).*

I have got a Master's degree in Business Administration.

He got his master's degree three years ago.

Mature student *[Noun] (a student at a college or university who's older than others).*

He studied law as a mature student.

There are many benefits to being a mature student.

Public schools *[Noun] (a school that is supported and paid for by the government).*

He was educated at a public school.

My son finished a public school a few years ago.

Schoolboy error *[Noun] (a very simple, basic and foolish mistake).*

Lucy made a schoolboy error on her English test.

Tom made a schoolboy error by accepting a lunch invitation from a journalist.

Single-sex schools *[Noun] (schools that have only one sex (for either boys or girls)).*

My sister happily attended a single-sex school for 6 years.

I would never send my kids to a single-sex school.

To attend classes *[Verb] (to go to classes).*

In European universities, students are not required to attend classes.

Do not waste your money on tuition if you are not even going to attend classes.

Some students may not be able to pass the test in class because they don't attend classes regularly.

To learn something by heart *[Verb] (to memorize something).*

You should try to learn by heart these English words and phrases.

The boy learned the poem by heart.

To meet a deadline *[Verb] (to finish something in time (by or before it is due)).*

I'm trying to meet a deadline.

Do you take personal responsibility for failing to meet a deadline?

To pass with flying colours *[Verb] (to achieve, or accomplish something very successfully).*

He is studying hard and he will pass IELTS with flying colours.

He passed his exams with flying colours.

She passed her job interview with flying colours.

To pursue studying *[Verb] (to follow a course (education)).*

Peter would like to pursue studies in the future to become a lawyer.

She wants to pursue studying after high school.

To take a year out *[Verb] (to spend one year working to gain more valuable experience).*

Many graduates want to take a year out to save the money they need to embark on a course of further study.

My son took a year out and went traveling to Japan.

She took a year out to travel around South America.

Concentrate *[Verb] (to give full your attention to something).*

He couldn't concentrate on his lessons. His mind was on other things.

You might need to concentrate on what you're reading in order to understand it.

If you make so much noise, I can't concentrate on my homework.

Distraction *[Noun] (something that prevents you from giving full attention to something else).*

He worked hard all morning, without distraction.

The baby's constant crying drove me to distraction.

My kids drive me to distraction at times.

Thesis *[Noun] (a long piece of writing that is submitted in support of candidature for an academic degree).*

Sarah has been working on her thesis for over a year and she still has lots of work to do.

Lucy wrote her doctoral thesis on contemporary Germany literature.

Assignment *[Noun] (work that you must do as part of a job or course of study).*

I'm feeling much more confident in doing my first college assignment.

He stayed up all night finishing his assignment.

The student apologized for handing in his assignment late due to his illness.

Controversy *[Noun] (a disagreement or argument about something)*.

His views have excited a lively controversy among fellow scientists.

His latest book has attracted a lot of controversy.

Theoretical *[Adjective] (based on theories or ideas that relate to a subject instead of on practical application)*.

The training is practical rather than theoretical.

The course is designed to be practical rather than theoretical.

To be poor at something *[Verb] (not to be good at something)*.

I am poor at drawing.

He is very poor at maths at school.

Certificate *[Noun] (an official document shows that an educational program has been completed)*.

The language certificate has three levels: basic, intermediate and advanced.

TOEFL, TOEIC and IELTS are English certificates which aim for academic use and are widely used around the world.

Diploma *[Noun] (a document given by a college or university to show that you have completed an educational program (finished your studies))*.

Have you actually seen Tom's diploma?

He is a commerce graduate with a diploma in computer applications.

Degree *[Noun] (the qualification that you get after completing a course of study at a university)*.

It took him six years to get his bachelor's degree in math.

My sister got her law degree in 2010.

To resit an exam *[Verb] (to take an examination again).*

The teacher forced him to resit the exam the week after.

Pupils who score less than 5 marks have to resit the test.

Skip classes *[Verb] (to miss a class or not go to a class for some reason).*

He often skips classes.

Bullied students tend to skip classes because they feel uncomfortable at school.

Memorable *[Adjective] (something or event that is easily remembered, usually because it is special or unusual).*

His wedding was a memorable event for all.

Graduation ceremony is a memorable event for all students.

Specialty *[Noun] (a special field of study).*

Her specialty is English literature.

His specialty is criminal law.

To gain *[Verb] (to receive, to get).*

An internship will help students gain experience.

Reading books is a way to gain knowledge.

Schedule *[Noun] (a plan for doing a list of things at certain times).*

He always has a full schedule.

She has been forced to adjust her schedule.

Inspiring *[Adjective] (to be exciting and makes someone feel strongly interested in).*

What he said at the meeting today was very inspiring.

I find these quotes very inspiring.

Rewarding *[Adjective] (providing someone with satisfaction, pleasure, or profit).*

Teaching young children is a challenging and rewarding job.

I find learning languages to be very rewarding.

Vocational training *[Noun] (training that emphasizes skills and knowledge required for a particular job).*

Although vocational training is career-oriented, a few types of professions require a college degree.

Unwind *[Adjective] (to relax after hours of hard work).*

Listening to music helps me to unwind after a busy day at work.

Meditation is a tool that can help people unwind and let go of stress.

Encouraging *[Adjective] (giving someone confidence or hope about something).*

He sent me an encouraging message.

A coach is encouraging his team.

Parents often use encouraging words to motivate their children to achieve high standards.

Strict *[Adjective] (if you are strict, you have definite rules and expect people to obey completely).*

Her English teacher is very strict.

Both of my parents are not strict with me.

Supportive *[Adjective] (giving someone support, encouragement, and advice).*

My girlfriend was very supportive when I was ill.

His boss was very supportive and gave him time off work.

Keep track of *[Verb] (to keep an eye on something).*

I can't keep track of the new music.

Bank statements help you keep track of where your money is going.

Strive *[Verb] (to make great efforts to achieve something)*.

We must strive to secure steady growth.

He strove very hard to remain calm.

Break *[Verb] (a short period of time for relaxation)*.

Let's take a short break.

We usually have a short break for lunch, then start to work again at 2 o'clock.

Sincerity *[Noun] (the fact of showing your honesty of mind)*.

He impressed her with his sincerity.

If you question her sincerity, do not ask for her help.

(To) disclose *[Verb] (to give someone or reveal information about something)*.

I can't disclose that information yet.

He disclosed to me that he had been in prison.

(To) recall *[Verb] (to remember something that happened in the past)*.

I can't recall his name at the moment.

I failed to recall the book's title.

A heavy workload *[Noun] (a large amount of work or many tasks to perform)*.

Due to the heavy workload, many employees suffer from depression.

He's struggling to cope with the heavy workload.

Bullying *[Verb] (using superior strength repeatedly and intentionally to frighten or hurt another person)*.

The older boy causes problems at school by bullying younger children.

Bullying isn't just done with kids, adults bully each other too.

Competent *[Adjective]* *(to be capable of doing something well)*.

Tom is regarded as the most competent employee.

She is a competent teacher.

Excel *[Verb]* *(to be extremely good at something)*.

He excels in sports and in many other activities.

Rebecca always excels in languages at school.

To fall behind with your studies *[Verb]* *(to progress more slowly in studying than other people)*.

These students regularly miss classes and fall behind with their studies.

To impose discipline *[Verb]* *(to make students obey the rules of a school or college)*.

The teacher misused his ability to impose discipline on his students.

Attendance record *[Noun]* *(a record of how often someone has been present at an event or an institution)*.

He has a good attendance record.

Lucy, who is a fine student, has a perfect attendance record.

Tertiary education/higher education *[Noun]* *(education for people at college or university level)*.

More than 50% of secondary school pupils going on to tertiary education.

Excessive alcohol used by tertiary education students is well documented.

To accumulate *[Verb]* *(to gather or collect something gradually as time passes)*.

He accumulated a large fortune by hard work.

People tend to spend a greater proportion of their incomes when they accumulate more wealth.

Bedtime reading *[Noun] (a book, novel etc read at bedtime).*

Bedtime reading with your child can have a fantastic effect on enhancing your child's attention span.

Bedtime reading helps get children to sleep.

Kindergarten = pre-school education *[Noun]*

Can you remember your kindergarten teacher's name?

He and I have been friends since kindergarten.

A native speaker *[Noun] (someone who has spoken a language since he/she was a baby and did not learn it as a foreign language).*

Speak like a native speaker by using sentence stress in English.

He doesn't think it's necessary for him to sound like a native speaker, he just wants to be able to speak fluently.

To have a good grasp of *[Verb] (to have a complete, clear understanding of something).*

He doesn't have a good grasp of the principles yet.

After taking a year-long computer course, Peter had a good grasp of computer programming.

WORK/ EMPLOYMENT

Eager beaver *[Noun] (someone who is extremely enthusiastic and works very hard).*

Being eager beaver, she sometimes is not well-liked by her colleagues.

Don't be such an eager beaver, we have a lot of time to complete the task.

Burden *[Noun] (a duty, responsibility, or something that causes worry, stress or hard work).*

Her illness placed a heavy financial burden on her family.

The tax system imposed a heavy financial burden on the factories.

Meet someone's needs *[Verb] (to satisfy someone's needs).*

He has a satisfying job, but it doesn't pay enough to meet his needs.

The job provided her with a good income to meet her needs for food, clothing, and accommodations.

Take on *[Verb] (to undertake; to accept to do something).*

He's not afraid to take on challenging work.

She has taken on the task of looking after her elderly mother.

Doable *[Adjective] (something is doable if it can be achieved or possible to do).*

Passing the reading and writing tests is doable.

His daughter didn't think her homework was doable, but she was just complaining and being lazy.

Career *[Noun] (the job or profession that you do during your working life).*

He was happy to have chosen a career that suited his personality perfectly.

The scandal ruined her career.

Deadline *[Noun]* *(a time when something is due or must be done/finished).*

He is having trouble meeting the deadline.

Because of her incompetence, we won't make our deadline.

Overtime *[Adverb]* *(beyond the usual time, extra time spent at work).*

He was forced to work overtime.

I'm afraid that he has to work overtime.

Probation *[Noun]* *(a period of time during which someone who has been given a new job is tested to see whether they are suitable for work).*

John has been hired for a period of probation of 6 months.

She was asked to work for a period of probation of 3 months.

Handle someone's workload *[Verb]* *(to manage the amount of work that someone has to do).*

He cannot handle his workload! He is stressing out!

She self-trained herself on programs that she thought would handle her workload more efficiently.

Handwork *[Noun]* *(the act of creating something with the hands and not by machines).*

Handwork activities such as knitting, embroidery, weaving, doll and puppet making, papermaking, etc.

I loved to do handwork activities when I was a teenager.

Out of steam *[Expression]* *(to lose energy, tired, exhausted).*

I am out of steam to finish setting up as it's been a hard week.

Due to today's intense workday, he is out of steam, so he won't be able to work tomorrow.

Applicant *[Noun] (someone who makes a formal request for a job).*

Applicants were requested to submit their resumes.

He was writing a professional letter to give his applicants the good news.

Dream career *[Noun] (a job/profession that someone desires to have).*

A dream career of being a doctor is what she wants to pursue in her academic studies.

Inspired by art, designing themed lands is his dream career.

Carry on *[Verb] (to continue to do something).*

She wants to carry on studying until her baby is born.

She doesn't want to come with me. She wants to carry on studying.

I'll carry on working until I'm 60.

Productivity *[Noun] (the quality of producing something).*

When I sit down to write, the most important factor in my productivity is a comfort.

His work productivity improves, and his stress level goes way down.

Observe *[Verb] (to watch, look at, see).*

The patient must be observed constantly.

The change is too small to be observed.

Ambition *[Noun] (a strong desire to do or to achieve something).*

His ambition is to own a helicopter.

My ambition is to become a jet pilot.

Manual work *[Noun] (work involving the hands and physical strength, as opposed to an office job).*

Sewing is manual work.

Gardening and manual work are a great pleasure to our children.

Retail staff *[Noun] (employees who sell products to the public).*

Retail staff are trained to communicate with customers.

They are employed as retail staff in a large store.

Collaborate *[Verb] (to work jointly with others to create or achieve something).*

He agreed to collaborate with her in writing his biography.

Follow in someone's footsteps *[Verb] (to do the same job or to have the same style of life as someone else).*

She followed in her father's footsteps and became a teacher.

Tom followed in his father's footsteps, starting his own business.

I collaborated with my daughter on the French translation of a text on food production.

Work things out *[Verb] (to find a solution).*

We help them to work things out.

Conflicts teach you how to compromise and work things out.

Manually *[Adverb] (by hand (not by machine)).*

The work was done manually, not by a machine.

You may need to enter this information manually.

Dedicated *[Adjective] (to be devoted or totally committed to something (a task or purpose)).*

My father is very dedicated to his work.

People who are dedicated to their jobs often achieve their professional goals.

Be willing to *[Verb] (to be ready or happy to do something if it is necessary).*

He was willing to admit he was wrong.

They are no longer willing to give us a discount.

She is willing to discuss the problem.

Sort out *[Verb] (to deal with your own, or someone else's, problems successfully).*

We need to get these problems sorted out as soon as possible.

I felt we sorted out a lot of problems.

Associate with *[Verb] (connect with).*

I don't associate with people like him.

As a manager of the company, it is difficult for him to associate with his employees outside the office on weekends.

Keep someone from doing something *[Verb] (to prevent, stop someone from doing something).*

His snoring kept me from falling asleep.

Illness kept him from attending the meeting.

Determined *[Adjective] (making a firm decision to do something and not to change it).*

He is a very determined person. He will get the job he wants.

His early failures made him even more determined to succeed.

By trial and error *[Expression] (to learn something from the mistakes that you make).*

Science progresses by trial and error.

He would simply have to learn by trial and error.

Stable *[Adjective] (firmly fixed (not likely to change)).*

He is in a stable condition after suffering multiple injuries.

The temperature is quite stable from day to day.

Day off *[Noun] (a day without going to work).*

I think she should have a day off soon. She can't keep going like this all the time.

You should take a day off.

Get the hang of *[Verb] (to understand the technique of how to operate or do (something)).*

I'm starting to get the hang of how this computer works.

It took him a few hours to get the hang of flying a kite.

Apply for *[Verb] (to enroll in; to write a letter asking for a job).*

He's applied for a job with an insurance company.

Seven people applied for the job, but none of them were employed.

Strides *[Noun] (advances or improvements in the way that something is progressing).*

A group of experts are making great strides in the search for a diabetes cure.

The government has made great strides in reducing poverty.

Experience *[Verb] (if you experience something, it happens to you, and affect your feeling).*

He experienced a feeling of deep sadness as he entered the refugee camp.

I experienced intense cold at the South Pole last year.

After the surgery, she experienced a lot of lethargy but no pain.

Dedicate *[Verb] (to devote your time and effort to someone or something).*

My mother dedicated every hour of the day to taking care of us while my father was away at sea.

He has dedicated all his life to helping poor people.

To confront *[Verb] (to deal with a problem or difficult situation).*

A soldier often has to confront danger.

She is confronted by many difficulties.

Hardship *[Noun] (a situation that is severe, difficult and unpleasant).*

The soldiers had to endure great hardship during the war.

He closed his eyes tightly and endured the pain.

Sacrifice *[Noun] (the act of giving up something important or valuable to you in order to do something else or to help someone).*

After his wife died, he made sacrifices to take care of his children.

He sacrificed his personal life in order to get ahead in his career.

Incentive *[Noun] (something that motivates or encourages you to do something).*

The workers have no incentive to work harder.

Tom had no incentive to work after he was refused a promotion.

Tension *[Noun] (the state of being stressed, nervous, or emotional strain).*

There was a lot of tension at the meeting.

There are growing tensions between the two countries.

Criticism *[Noun] (the act of expressing disapproval of someone or something).*

She ignored the criticisms of her friends.

The plan has attracted criticism from the consumer group.

To be engrosséd in something *[Verb]* (to be completely focused on something).

She seemed completely engrossed in her work.

Mary was so engrossed in the book that she forgot the cakes in the oven.

To recharge one's energy *[Verb] (to recover your strength by resting for a time).*

We enjoyed a week away at the coast and recharged our energy.

She went back out to sea to recharge her energy.

Career advancement *[Noun] (development in jobs).*

We congratulated the employee on his career advancement.

Lifelong learning is essential to career advancement.

Diligence *[Noun] (careful and determined in your work).*

I praised him for his diligence.

She is diligent in her studies.

To earn a living *[Verb] (to earn money).*

He used to earn a living as a musician, but now he is a photographer.

She earns a living as a writer.

Play an essential part IN something *[Expression] (have an important role in something).*

He plays an essential part in running the business smoothly.

Tom plays an essential part in this project.

Determination *[Noun] (the quality that makes someone continue trying to do something).*

I admired him for his determination.

She always shows great determination in everything she undertakes.

Perseverance *[Noun] (the effort to do or achieve something in spite of difficulties and* *obstacles).*

I was surprised by her perseverance.

There's no success without perseverance.

Overcome *[Verb] (to succeed in dealing with a problem or difficulty that has been preventing you from achieving something).*

We have to overcome many difficulties.

He overcame injury to win the Olympic gold medal.

To acquire experience/knowledge/skill *[Verb] (to gain experience/knowledge/skill by your own efforts).*

I try to acquire knowledge by reading books every evening.

Students acquire skills for advanced level English writing.

To move up the career ladder *[Verb] (a series of actions you have taken to make progress in your career).*

He can move up the career ladder in his current position.

She rapidly moved up the career ladder becoming a financial analyst.

Commitment *[Noun] (the willingness to work hard or to be dedicated to a job or an activity).*

We've always had a commitment to customer service, and we keep working to improve.

We had a commitment to enriching the lives of our children.

(To) proceed *[Adjective] (to begin or continue an action or process).*

The district attorney is unwilling to proceed due to insufficient evidence.

I would like to know how you will proceed in this matter.

Self-motivated *[Adjective] (to be capable of hard work without the need for encouragement).*

People who are self-motivated tend to be more organized and more self-esteem.

He is highly self-motivated, productive and successful.

Demanding *[Adjective] (needing a lot of effort or attention).*

My job is quite demanding at times, but I really enjoy it.

The work of a farmer is physically very demanding.

Work on *[Verb] (try hard to repair or improve something).*

You need to work on your pronunciation every day if you want to pass the exam.

She is working on getting fit before the wedding.

Job prospects *[Noun] (the possibility of being successful and having more opportunities at work).*

After he graduated top of his class at Harvard, his job prospects looked great.

People with qualifications and experience usually have the best job prospects.

She becomes immensely disappointed and lies to her family about the sanguinity of her job prospects.

Work environment *[Noun] (the surrounding conditions in which you work in).*

What is your ideal work environment?

If you want to improve your work experience, you should have a good work environment around you.

Job satisfaction *[Noun] (a feeling of enjoyment that you derives from your job).*

When he chooses a career, job satisfaction is always the most important factor.

Some employees are more interested in job satisfaction than in earning high salaries.

Levels of job satisfaction have increased over the last few years.

Employee *[Noun] (a person who is paid to work for another person or an organization).*

Each employee was given a bonus.

As an employee of our company, he is automatically entitled to a special discount.

(Be) occupied with *[Adjective] (be busy with something).*

He was fully occupied with driving.

She was occupied with household work.

Works of craftsmanship *[Noun] (objects made by people who are very skilled at making things by hand).*

Jewelry made to a special design, furniture, clothing, or cutlery can all be called works of craftsmanship.

The museums of every city are full of beautiful works of craftsmanship made by skilled workers in past centuries.

To work/ perform miracles *[Verb] (to achieve extraordinary/very good results).*

We need a marketing team that can perform miracles to bring the company back to its former glory.

His exercise program has worked miracles for him.

She worked miracles with the redecorating.

White-collar *[Noun] (relating to the work done or those who work in an office, not a factory).*

White-collar workers now work longer hours.

She has a white-collar job as an accountant at one of the largest finance firms in London.

The world of work *[Noun] (the job market; types of work and the possibilities for employment).*

Certain qualities are important to succeed in the world of work, for example, honesty and hard work.

The world of work is changing - more women are leaving home to find jobs and pursue a career.

Western styles of clothing are a positive development. They are practical and affordable in the modern world of work and leisure.

Make an honest living *[Verb] (to earn money through hard work).*

She makes an honest living by working at the bakery during the week.

Although he was a criminal, now he makes an honest living as an assistant in a supermarket.

Make ends meet *[Verb] (to earn enough money to buy the things you need without getting into debt).*

Elderly people can make ends meet on their pensions.

Many students have a difficult time trying to make ends meet.

Cope with *[Verb] (deal successfully with something difficult).*

It must be difficult for her to cope with five small children and a job.

After the divorce, she had to cope with a full-time job and the raising of her two kids.

Devote to *[Verb] (give a large amount of time or attention to someone or something).*

Nowadays, children devote much of their free time to playing electronic games or using the Internet.

She devotes too much time to her job; she should spend more time with her family.

He seems to devote all her efforts to his career.

Huge challenge *[Noun]* *(very big challenge; it's difficult or tough).*

Raising children could be a huge challenge for older parents.

Reading such texts can be a huge challenge, but an important one.

Future workforce *[Noun]* *(workers in the future).*

The future workforce will face new challenges that they never experienced before.

Providing opportunities for young people to work is very important in developing the future workforce.

Job-hunting = job seeking, or job searching *[Noun]* *(the act of looking for a job).*

Tom wants to go job hunting.

He was job-hunting for 6 months before he finally found employment in a car factory.

Workload *[Noun]* *(the amount of work that has to be done by a particular person in a period of time).*

Tom's struggling to cope with the heavy workload.

I've had an increased workload this year.

To job share *[Verb]* *(to share the responsibilities and the pay of a single full-time job between two people).*

They both want to job share.

It is easier for managers to job share or work part-time while they have young children.

Flexible working hours *[Noun]* *(a flexible schedule allows an employee to work hours that can be changed by agreement between the employer and the employee).*

Flexible working hours could give working parents more time to spend with their children.

Most employees would prefer more flexible working hours.

Sweated labour *[Noun] (hard work that is done by people who work for long hours for low wages in poor conditions).*

The mill owners used sweated labour to earn them fortunes.

Sweated Labour are often categorised by factors such as poor education, and language.

Guest workers *[Noun] (people, usually from a poor country, are permitted to live and work temporarily in a richer country).*

We have not been a country which has used guest workers.

Germany is accustomed to receiving visitors and guest workers from foreign countries.

Dead-end job *[Noun] (a job that has no prospects of promotion).*

She was stuck in a dead-end job for nearly 6 years.

Custodial work and waitressing are definitely dead-end jobs.

(To) make a living *[Verb] (to make money to pay for the things that you need in life such as housing, food, etc).*

She made a living by working as a cook.

Many young people like to make a living in big cities.

Life skills *[Noun] (skills that are necessary, useful or important in everyday life).*

Job skills allow you to do a particular job and life skills help you through everyday tasks.

Teamwork and problem-solving are life skills.

Transferable skills *[Noun] (skills that are used in different jobs or different situations).*

Transferable skills are the key to professional success.

Transferable skills can be a great help if you don't have much experience of work.

Level of competition *[Noun] (the extent, or degree of a competition).*

The level of competition in this class is getting more intense.

Paperwork *[Noun] (written or clerical work that involves producing reports, keeping records, and writing letters).*

She sat down again and buried herself in paperwork.

The organization offers practical help in dealing with paperwork.

Work experience *[Noun] (the experience and skills that you gain while working in a specific field or occupation).*

His work experience is limited.

Do you have work experience?

He doesn't have any work experience.

Career woman *[Noun] (a woman who considers her job is very important in her life).*

She wants him to respect her as a career woman.

She is an ambitious career woman.

Colleague *[Noun] (a fellow employee who works in the same organization, profession or department as you).*

Tom and his colleague are going to work on the project all weekend.

My colleagues assured me that I had done nothing wrong.

She was recommended for the post by a colleague.

Client *[Noun] (someone using the services of a professional person or organization such as a doctor or lawyer).*

The client asked us to begin this project.

Merchants receive either money or trade goods with their clients.

One of our clients provides an online consumer information service.

Retire *[Verb] (leave one's job and cease to work because of old age or ill health).*

He will retire from the army next year.

He was forced to retire early from teaching because of ill health.

Trainee *[Noun] (someone who is learning and practicing the skills of a particular profession or job).*

He joined the company as a graduate trainee.

The trainee pilot flew his first solo today.

Training course *[Noun] (a course providing training in a particular field or profession).*

It was a great training course that covered everything you need to know about Microsoft Excel!

Freelance *[Noun] (working for different companies at different times rather than working all the time for a single organization).*

He's been freelance for several years.

Most of the journalists I know work freelance.

Well-paid *[Adjective] (earning or receiving a good amount of money for work).*

I have an interesting, well-paid job, with opportunities to travel.

He has got a well-paid job and can afford to live in a beautiful house.

Pay rise *[Noun] (an increase in your salary for doing your job).*

He is expecting to be given a pay-rise next month.

What would I need to do to receive the pay rise I was looking for?

Sick pay *[Noun] (money that you are given by an employer when you are unable to* *work because of illness).*

How much sick pay do employees receive?

Tom has no sick pay, no paid vacation and no paid overtime.

Working environment *[Noun] (location where a task is completed).*

What would be your ideal working environment?

He has a stressful job in a bad working environment.

Dream job *[Noun] (a job that you love to do).*

Her dream job would be to work as an actress.

His dream job is to be a pilot.

Prospects *[Noun] (the possibility or likelihood that something good will happen in the future).*

He had more prospects of success than others.

It's a great career with good promotion prospects.

Engaging *[Adjective] (attractive, pleasant and charming).*

He was very engaging with the audience.

The seminar was very engaging.

Daily routine *[Noun] (the usual set of activities that you do at a particular time).*

My mother is getting tired of her daily routine.

The old woman has an attendant who helps her with her daily routine.

I'm fed up with my daily routine.

In charge of *[Verb] (to have control over or responsibility for something or someone).*

The teacher is in charge of the class.

He's in charge of the department.

Job opportunity *[Noun]* *(an opportunity of employment).*

Don't waste time and miss out on your ideal job opportunity.

I'm excited about this job opportunity.

An occupation *[Noun]* *(a job).*

His occupation is a doctor so he earns a lot of money.

Her occupation is a teacher.

Profession *[Noun]* *(a type of job that requires special skills and qualifications to do).*

His profession is a teacher though his occupation (or his job right now) is an actor.

Teaching English is his profession.

She reached the heights of her profession at the age of 35.

Workplace *[Noun]* *(a place, such as an office or factory where you work).*

Smoking is not permitted in the workplace.

Sexism and racism are still rampant in today's workplace.

Salary *[Noun]* *(a fixed regular amount of money that you earn each month from your job).*

I'm satisfied with my salary.

She is not content with her present salary.

Unemployed *[Noun]* *(without a job; not having a job).*

She's been unemployed for over a year.

The unemployed are a growing portion of the population.

Promotion *[Noun]* *(the act of raising someone to a higher ranking position at a workplace).*

He didn't work hard enough for a promotion.

He'll look for another job if he doesn't get the promotion.

A workaholic *[Noun] (a person who spends most of their time working and finds it difficult not to work).*

Her father is a workaholic.

Mary spends too much time at the office. She's such a workaholic.

To be in charge of *[Verb] (to have control over someone or something and have responsibility for them).*

He is in charge of the municipal housing project.

She is in charge of a group of ten people in her department.

To deal with *[Verb] (to take action in order to solve a problem).*

We've got bigger problems to deal with.

I have a situation that I have to deal with at the moment.

To involve *[Verb] (to contain/ to include).*

Proper exercise involves physical as well as mental discipline.

He tends to shy away from anything that involves public speaking.

Does your current job involve traveling?

HEALTH/ KEEPING FIT

Refresh *[Verb] (to make someone less tired or hot).*

A glass of orange juice refreshed me after a long walk.

A cup of coffee refreshed me.

Energetic *[Adjective] (to be full of energy).*

He isn't as energetic as he once was.

He seemed a dynamic and energetic leader.

Boost someone's immune system *[Verb] (to make someone's physical health stronger in order to fight against illness).*

I was recommended seven natural remedies to help me boost my immune system.

A healthy diet of fruit and vegetables, combined with exercise will help you boost your immune system.

Suffer *[Verb] (to experience physical or mental pain (a disease, pain, sadness, etc.)).*

He is suffering from a headache.

I was suffering from fever.

Ageing *[Noun] (the process of becoming older and less healthy).*

Many skin care products claim to stop the ageing process nowadays.

Exposure to the sun can accelerate the ageing process.

The ageing population.

Awareness *[Noun] (the state of knowing and understanding that something is happening).*

The accident has raised the public's awareness of the importance of wearing a helmet.

Fit *[Verb] (to be the right shape or size for someone or something).*

This shirt fits me well.

The suit fits him perfectly.

Healthy *[Adjective] (to be good for health).*

My grandfather is very healthy.

He appears to be strong and healthy.

Sanitation *[Noun] (the process of keeping places clean and healthy, especially by removing human waste).*

People who work in sanitation help to keep our communities clean and beautiful.

A lack of clean water and sanitation were the main problems.

By improving sanitation in the city, the authorities were able to reduce the impact of some serious diseases.

Antioxidant *[Adjective] (a substance which inhibits oxidation and slows down the aging process).*

An antioxidant keeps a substance from degrading or decaying.

Vitamin C is good to prevent illness because it has antioxidant properties.

Respiratory *[Adjective] (relating to or connected with breathing).*

She suffers from a respiratory disease.

Our lungs are a main part of the respiratory system.

Detoxify *[Verb] (to remove toxic or poisonous substances out of your body).*

Seaweed baths can help to detoxify the body.

Her cells are dying every day and need to detoxify to live longer.

Build up *[Verb] (to make someone healthier and stronger).*

After the operation, he ate lots of fruit and vegetables to build up his strength.

He has always been encouraged to swim to build up the strength of his muscles.

Soothe one's soul *[Verb] (to make us feel relaxed and peaceful).*

Would you like to sing me a song to soothe my soul?

We stopped and let the sight soothe our soul.

My sister has just bought a condo in Sydney.

Life-threatening *[Adjective] (be highly likely to cause death/ kill someone).*

Her mother has a life-threatening illness.

There are hundreds of life-threatening diseases lurking around us.

Fatal *[Adjective] (causing or leading to death).*

He is the person who caused a fatal accident.

Hepatitis is a potentially fatal disease.

Immune system *[Noun] (the bodily system that protects the body from infection and disease).*

The immune system does a great job of keeping people healthy and preventing infections.

Look after *[Verb] (to take care of (someone or something)).*

He looked after my dog while I was out.

The kids are being looked after by their grandparents.

To be detrimental to health *[Adjective] (to be damaging or harmful to health).*

Poor eating habits are detrimental to health.

Smoking can be detrimental to health.

A fitness regime *[Noun] (a habit of taking regular exercise).*

Her doctor has put her on a special fitness regime to help her get back to good health.

He has a new fitness regime to strengthen his back.

Exhausted *[Adjective] (very tired).*

She was too exhausted and distressed to talk about the tragedy.

You must be exhausted after your weekend.

The young boys were totally exhausted after playing football all afternoon.

Remedy *[Noun] (a solution to a particular problem).*

Herbal remedies for aches and pains.

She took a herbal remedy for her hay fever.

To remedy *[Verb] (to correct or improve something).*

I plan to remedy the empty stomach very soon.

The loans are provided to remedy the failings of the decent homes standard.

Seasick *[Adjective] (to vomit or feel sick because of the movement of the ship or boat).*

She felt seasick as the little boat bounced up and down over the waves.

I never had any experience being seasick but I feel seasick now.

Take care of *[Verb] (to treat someone or something carefully so that he/she/it stays in good condition).*

I'll take care of him.

He took care of a ten-room house without help.

Relieve pressure on *[Verb] (remove or reduce pressure on someone or something).*

This will relieve pressure on the trains to some extent.

In order to relieve pressure on students, the exams were replaced by continual assessment.

Pass away *[Verb] (to die).*

The old man passed away last night. He had cancer.

I'm so sorry to hear that her father passed away.

Strain *[Noun] (mental pressure or worry caused by a difficult situation).*

He sometimes finds it a strain to be responsible for the mortgage with only a part-time job.

The repayments for his new car are putting a strain on his finances.

Detrimental *[Adjective] (bad, negative).*

The habit of smoking cigarette is detrimental to people's physical well-being.

The alcohol in beer is detrimental to your health.

Adverse *[Adjective] (negative, harmful, unfavourable and unpleasant).*

Her headache had an adverse effect on her performance in the exam.

Dirt and disease are adverse to the best growth of children.

Pose potential health risks *[Adjective] (bring some risks).*

Contaminated drinking water would pose potential health risks.

This food can pose potential health risks.

Check-ups *[Noun] (check your health).*

He goes to her doctor for regular check-ups.

My parents have health checks and dental check-ups.

Longevity *[Noun]* *(long life; living for a long time).*

I wish you longevity and good health.

The dog has a longevity of about ten years.

Be out of condition *[Expression]* *(not be healthy or fit due to lack of exercise.)*

Many people are out of condition due to the lack of exercise.

If you don't want to be out of condition, you must exercise regularly.to be out of condition.

Get into shape *[Expression]* *(to become strong, fit and healthy/ to be in good physical condition.)*

If you don't exercise regularly, you won't get into shape.

Tom wants to get into shape, so he's started working out every day.

On safety grounds *[Expression]* *(for reasons of safety).*

The building was closed on safety grounds.

To exert oneself *[Verb]* *(to make a big physical effort to do something).*

He is an excellent player, so he hardly even had to exert herself to beat me.

He didn't want to exert himself on such a hot day.

Take up regular exercise *[Verb]* *(to learn or start doing exercise regularly as a habit.)*

Her mother always encourages her to take up regular exercise.

You are a bit overweight, so you should go on a diet and take up regular exercise.

Extreme sports *[Noun]* *(a sporting activity which is very dangerous and exciting).*

Base jumping is an extreme sport.

A lot of extreme sports are popular in New Zealand.

Jogging *[Noun] (the activity of running at a steady, gentle speed).*

Since she started jogging, she's lost three and a half inches from her waistline.

I like jogging early in the morning.

Do aerobics/ yoga *[Verb] (very active physical exercises, often performed while listening to music).*

I do aerobics and weight training at the gym.

Children can do yoga anytime and anyplace.

I do yoga twice a week.

To be addicted to *[Adjective] (to be unable to stop doing something as a habit).*

He's addicted to drugs.

She's addicted to junk food.

A sedentary lifestyle *[Noun] (an inactive lifestyle with little exercise or physical activity).*

She took her medicine, but her bad eating habits and sedentary lifestyle hampered her recovery.

Nowadays, a sedentary lifestyle is becoming increasingly popular in spite of a big number of sports facilities.

A team player *[Noun] (someone who willingly cooperates with others in a team, or group).*

Employers expect employees to be team players.

Employers want to hire people who are good team players.

Have a go *[Verb] (to try or attempt to do something)*

I've never sat on a horse so far, but I'll have a go.

She'd like to have a go at playing the piano.

Thoroughness *[Noun] (the act of doing something very carefully and with great attention to detail).*

I appreciate the thoroughness of her report.

I admired his thoroughness, and his understanding of the psychiatric process.

Lifestyle *[Noun] (the way in which a person lives).*

He changed his lifestyle completely after his fatal heart attack.

They lived a very lavish lifestyle.

Alleviate *[Verb] (to make something less severe).*

The man hopes these things will alleviate his headache.

The doctor gave her an injection to alleviate the pain.

To flourish *[Verb] (to grow or develop in a healthy or successful way).*

The fertile ground and ample water supply will allow the crops to flourish.

The arts began to flourish at that time.

To take up sport *[Expression] (to start doing sport).*

Many young people took up sport as an occupation.

More and more men, women and children took up sport for fun.

Physical fitness *[Noun] (good health and strength achieved through sports, occupations, daily activities, and exercise).*

He is most different when it comes to his physical fitness.

She set goals for improving her physical fitness.

Today we're going to do a physical fitness test.

Stamina *[Noun] (physical or mental strength that enables someone to sustain prolonged physical or mental effort).*

He needs stamina to be a long-distance runner.

She had the strength and a lot of stamina to take the lead and win the gold medal.

In good shape *[Expression] (in a good physical condition).*

Her boyfriend is in good shape.

He is in good shape for the marathon.

She is in good shape for a woman of her age.

Burn a lot of calories *[Expression] (to use up a lot of energy).*

Running an hour every morning in the park will burn a lot of calories.

You can burn a lot of calories with exercise in a short amount of time.

Flexibility *[Noun] (the ability to move and bend your body easily).*

Gumby was known for his flexibility, bending and twisting his entire body with ease.

Her great strength lies in her flexibility.

Meditation *[Noun] (thinking deeply in silence, to make you feel calm).*

He hit on the plan after long meditation.

I often try meditation after a stressful day at work to relax myself.

Well-being *[Noun] (health, happiness, and prosperity).*

They are trying hard to improve their well-being.

The care and well-being of patients should always come first.

Obese *[Adjective] (extremely fat or overweight (having excessive body fat))*.

Obese people tend to find it very difficult to stop overeating.

Being obese and lazy is dangerous to health.

To provide someone with a healthy diet *[Verb] (to give someone a diet which is healthy)*.

They need us to provide them with a healthy diet, fresh water, and shelter.

For a healthy and happy pet, you have to provide them with a healthy diet.

(To) endure *[Verb] (to experience and suffer something that is painful or unpleasant)*.

No matter how hard his opponent hit, the boxer was determined to endure the fight.

Students usually have to endure a lot of pressure during exam time.

Mature *[Adjective] (fully grown (behaving like an adult))*.

John is very mature for his age.

Lucy is only 6 years old, but she is very mature for her age and is often mistaken for a 10-year-old.

A sports fan *[Noun] (a person who is really interested in sport)*.

I am lucky to have the opportunity to interact with thousands of sports fans at the stadium.

After games, thousands of sports fans take to the Internet to blog about the game they were watching.

The Olympic stadium was filled with thousands of sports fans, eager to watch the final events.

To keep fit *[Verb] (to stay in good physical condition)*.

He keeps fit by jogging every morning.

To keep fit, I go jogging every Sunday with my friend.

To work out at the gym *[Expression] (to train the body through physical exercise at the gym).*

I work out at the gym every Sunday.

He works out at the gym five to seven hours a day.

Energize *[Verb] (to make someone feel energetic or enthusiastic).*

We felt very energized after our holiday.

I felt more energized after a bit of exercise.

To take regular exercise *[Verb] (to do some physical activity on a regular basis to improve health and fitness).*

She has a healthy diet and takes regular exercise.

I used to take regular exercise by hiking or cycling in the countryside.

Mental health problem *[Noun] (related to the physical illness of one's mind).*

He can't leave home because of his mental health problem.

He was not aware of his mental health problem.

To take gentle exercise *[Verb] (to do exercise which does not involve a lot of force or effort).*

We keep fit by taking gentle exercise, like jogging or even a walk in the park.

He gains strength daily; takes gentle exercise, and enjoys his food.

Chronic illness = chronic disease *[Noun] (a disease that persists for a long time and is difficult to cure).*

Vegetarians have a tendency to lower the risks of developing several chronic illnesses such as diabetes, heart disease, obesity and cancer.

Children with chronic illnesses may be ill at any given time.

Diabetes *[Noun]* *(a chronic disease that affects your body's ability to produce a lot of urine and feel thirsty)*.

He can't eat cake because he suffers from diabetes.

She suffers from diabetes and is unable to work.

Some people who suffer from diabetes have to take medicine every day.

Obesity *[Noun]* *(the fact of being very fat, in an unhealthy way)*.

Obesity can increase the risk of heart disease.

Obesity is attributable to a poor diet and a lack of exercise.

Vaccines *[Noun]* *(substances that are put into the blood to prevent someone from getting the disease)*.

Vaccines deliver antibodies that fight disease.

Measles vaccines were given to all the children in the school.

Basic necessities *[Noun]* *(the things necessary or indispensable which we must have and cannot survive without such as food, shelter, and other necessities of life)*.

People living in some countries do not even have the basic necessities of life.

Many people cannot even afford basic necessities, such as food and clothing.

Sufferings *[Noun]* *(the state of undergoing pain and unhappiness)*.

We cannot watch the sufferings of other people without wishing to help them.

This medicine helps to alleviate the sufferings of the patient.

Voluntary activities *[Noun]* *(activities that people do on a voluntary basis, without getting paid, they do it volunteers)*.

Good citizens participate in a variety of voluntary activities throughout the year.

Prisoners are engaged in a variety of voluntary activities in prison.

To build muscle *[Verb] (to gain muscle mass).*

Yoga won't build my muscles.

He is starting to walk now and wants to build his muscles.

Football fan *[Noun] (someone who likes football).*

I'm a football fan.

He is a football fan.

Football season *[Noun] (a period when football is played).*

During the second week of autumn, football season begins.

The British football season begins in August and ends in May.

Sports centre (fitness centre) *[Noun] (a specific building where people can play different sports and other activities).*

My brother practices fencing at a local sports centre.

The sports centre staff are lovely and really helpful.

Sports facilities *[Noun] (the equipment and services for doing sports).*

Indoor and outdoor sports facilities.

I chose this gym because it offers a wide range of sports facilities.

Champion *[Noun] (someone who wins the first prize in a competition; a winner).*

After winning all the matches, he became the champion.

I think that the Liverpool football team will be the champion this year.

To warm up *[Verb] (to perform light exercises before doing a sport).*

If you don't warm up before taking exercise, you risk injuring yourself.

I usually warm up 10 mins before doing exercises.

Maintain *[Verb] (to take care of and make something stay the same).*

She has found it difficult to maintain a healthy weight.

He tries to maintain healthy eating habits every day.

Vitamin C helps maintain healthy connective tissue.

Nutrients *[Noun] (a substance in food that provides nourishment essential for plants, animals, and people to live and grow).*

You need more nutrients in your diet.

Fresh fruit provides many nutrients such as vitamin C.

Overweight *[Adjective] (excessive or extra weight (heavier than you should be)).*

Tom's a bit overweight, but formerly he was quite a good athlete.

He's overweight and bald, yet somehow, he's incredibly attractive.

She is overweight and out of condition.

Health benefits *[Noun] (great advantages for health).*

Drinking tea has many health benefits.

This is a detailed article about the health benefits of fish.

Health Benefits of Yoga.

Health problems *[Noun] (things that have bad effects on someone's health).*

She has chronic health problems.

People with disabilities may suffer more health problems.

Mental health problems can affect anyone at any age.

In good health *[Expression] (to be healthy).*

I think it's necessary to sleep well to keep in good health.

My grandparents were in good health the last time I saw them.

I hope you are in good health.

In poor health *[Expression]* *(to be unhealthy)*.

He has been in poor health ever since he caught a flu last year.

She continued to carry out her duty although she was in poor health.

Allergy *[Noun]* *(a physical reaction to some specific food or substances)*.

His allergy is life-threatening.

His parents hope that he will grow out of his allergy one day.

Her allergy to the eye drops caused the ocular swelling.

The pediatrician gave my daughter an injection for her allergy.

Infection *[Noun]* *(a disease that is caused by bacteria or viruses)*.

Her ear infection caused her acute pain.

The polluted waters of the lake causes an infection in the children's eyes.

Vulnerable *[Adjective]* *(to be easily physically, emotionally, or mentally hurt)*.

Children are the most vulnerable members of society.

The elderly are particularly vulnerable to the flu.

Sedentary lifestyle *[Noun]* *(lifestyle with little or no physical activity)*.

As a result of her sedentary lifestyle, Jenna has gained a lot of weight.

People in sedentary jobs need to take exercise.

Cut down on *[Verb]* *(to reduce an amount of something)*.

The office is trying to cut down on electricity consumption.

We tried to cut down on the money we were spending on entertainment.

Nervous breakdown *[Noun]* *(a serious mental illness resulting from severe depression, insomnia, and anxiety)*.

If Peter does not rest more, he may have a nervous breakdown.

She suffered a nervous breakdown.

He is on the verge of a nervous breakdown.

Plastic surgery *[Noun] (operation to reshape, remodel or resize body parts, especially by the transfer of tissue, either in the treatment of injury or for cosmetic reasons).*

He needed plastic surgery on his face.

A lot of women use plastic surgery to make themselves more attractive to men.

Sick leave *[Noun] (paid absence from work because of illness).*

She has been on sick leave for seven months.

There are no paid holidays or sick leave if you are self-employed.

Common cold *[Noun] (a slight illness that a lot of people catch with symptoms like sneezing, coughing, runny nose and temperature).*

The common cold is found everywhere in the world.

She doctored herself for just a common cold.

Cancer *[Noun] (an extremely serious disease typically caused by a group of abnormal cells in a part of the body).*

Smoking can double the risk of lung cancer.

Nearly 3.5 million cases of skin cancer are treated each year.

Childhood diseases *[Noun] (illnesses such as Mumps, Chickenpox, Measles, etc. typically caught in childhood).*

He treats childhood diseases.

Vaccinations help prevent childhood diseases.

Addict *[Noun] (a person who likes doing or using something, especially something harmful).*

He is a TV addict and watches as much as he can.

Many young boys become computer addicts.

A check-up [Noun] (an examination done by a doctor to make sure that you are healthy).

The doctor gave him a thorough check-up.

I'm at the hospital having a check-up.

She felt ill for a few days, so she went for a check-up.

A runny nose [Noun] (a nose that has more liquid than it is usual).

He has a sore throat and runny nose.

I developed a bad cough and a runny nose after watching the football game in the pouring rain.

Chronic disease [Noun] (a type of disease that persists over a long period of time).

My grandfather suffers from a chronic disease.

Tom has a relative who suffers from a chronic disease and must take a range of medicines.

Painkillers [Noun] (a type of medicine that relieves pain).

Thinking she was starting a cold, she took some painkillers.

When I woke up, he was in so much pain that he took some painkillers.

To diagnose [Verb] (to recognise a physical or mental problem by examining the patient).

His father was diagnosed with a brain tumor last year.

The child had been diagnosed with asthma.

To stutter [Verb] (to talk the sounds of words over and over again in an uncontrolled way).

He stutters sometimes when he's excited;

He tended to stutter, which tried her patience.

Alive and kicking *[Adjective] (healthy and active).*

My grandfather is almost 90 but he's still alive and kicking.

She's all right, still alive and kicking.

To break a habit *[Verb] (to stop doing something that you do regularly, especially something bad or harmful).*

He broke his habit of smoking last year.

It can be hard to break a habit.

To black out *[Verb] (to suddenly lose consciousness).*

He blacked out and collapsed on the floor.

He drank 5 glasses of whisky and then he blacked out.

To be under the weather *[Expression] (do not feel well; feel sick).*

Tom was feeling a bit under the weather today, so he chose to take the day off.

I'm feeling a bit under the weather. I think I've caught a cold.

To phone in sick *[Expression] (to call your superior to inform him/her that you are too ill to go to work).*

I phoned in sick to let my boss know I wouldn't be coming in.

He had to phone in sick last week, because he caught a cold.

Sick as a dog = to be at death's door *[Expression] (very sick; extremely ill).*

I caught a flu and for three days I was as sick as a dog.

She can't come in to work today, she's sick as a dog.

White as a sheet *[Expression] (very pale, usually due to illness, shock, or fear).*

She went as white as a sheet when she heard the news.

On the plane, I noticed she was white as a sheet.

Take a nap = have a nap *[Verb] (to have a short period of sleep, especially during the day).*

I take a nap almost every day after lunch.

I had a nap for about an hour.

Relax *[Verb] (to take it easy; to calm down; to release tension and anxiety).*

I like to take a bath to relax after a hard day at work.

People in the 21st century worked hard and didn't have time to relax.

To set aside some time *[Verb] (to take some time).*

We set aside some time to discuss the new project.

If you don't have a pet, set aside some time to do exercise.

Take up *[Verb] (start to learn or do something).*

He decided to take up photography as a hobby.

She took up jogging after her doctor advised her to get some exercise.

Take part *[Verb] (participate (in something)).*

He took part in the sporting event.

We took part in the contest.

Be in the mood *[Expression] (to feel like doing something).*

I'm in the mood to listen to music online.

I'm not in the mood to talk to him.

Tend to *[Adverb] (usually, regularly or frequently).*

When he is tired, he tends to make mistakes.

She is really careful about what she eats because she tends to gain weight easily.

(To) have a stroll *[Verb] (to have a short walk to somewhere in a leisurely and relaxed way).*

We had a stroll at night along the beach.

My favorite pastime is having a stroll along the shore.

Rock climbing *[Noun] (the activity of climbing rocky cliffs, as a hobby or sport).*

People who enjoy rock climbing are adventurous and brave.

Rock-climbing is pretty popular these days.

Hiking *[Noun] (the activity of going on long walks in the countryside, usually for pleasure or exercise).*

I love hiking.

We'll get in some fishing and hiking and perhaps some hunting.

Do-It-Yourself *[Adjective] (also known as DIY, the activity of doing or making something without any support or assistance).*

A do-it-yourself kit for building a radio.

A do-it-yourself book.

Barely *[Adverb] (scarcely, hardly).*

Tom hurt his leg and can barely walk.

They barely had time to rescue the children from the burning apartment.

Fast-paced *[Adjective] (moving or happening very quickly; very busy).*

The show is very fast paced and the talent is outstanding.

Our shop is very fast paced and we require someone who can work well in the fast-paced environment.

The author's writing style is very fast-paced.

On cloud 9 *[Expression] (to be extremely happy)*.

Every time he calls me a scientist, I feel like I am on cloud nine.

I am on cloud nine in my new car.

Sedentary *[Adjective] ((of a person) tending to spend a lot of time sitting down and little physical exercise)*.

People who have a sedentary lifestyle are not very active.

Tom's computer programming job kept him sedentary for most of the day.

She has a sedentary job, working as a secretary in an office.

Every so often = from time to time *[Adverb] (occasionally; sometimes)*.

I meet him at the club every so often.

Every so often he treats himself to a meal in an expensive restaurant.

As a rule *[Adverb] (usually, but not always)*.

As a rule, we go shopping on Friday nights.

As a rule, my mom gets up at six o'clock, but yesterday morning she got up at eight.

Frequently *[Adverb] (regularly; often)*.

Tom used Skype frequently because he was overseas.

We wrote letters to each other frequently.

Give up *[Verb] (to quit; to stop doing something)*.

He was right to give up smoking.

I hope he won't give up playing football.

Talent *[Noun] (a special ability or skill that someone has)*.

He has a talent for public speaking.

He has a talent for painting.

She has a talent for dancing.

Flexible *[Adjective] (to be able to change or be changed easily)*.

My schedule for the weekend is very flexible.

Ballet dancers and yoga instructors are quite flexible.

Daily routine *[Noun] (activities that you do every day)*.

He is quite tired of/fed up with his daily routine.

My sister has an attendant who helps her with her daily routine.

Pursue one's passions *[Verb] (to follow your interests and desires)*.

He wants to pursue his passion for painting.

She has returned to pursue her passion for teaching English.

Rarely = seldom *[Adverb] (not very often)*.

He rarely plays any sports.

She rarely left the house and lived in the library.

She rarely goes out.

Adopt the habit *[Verb] (to begin to do something regularly)*.

She had adopted the habit of bowing in the manner of the Japanese.

After his wife's death, he had adopted the habit of smoking.

Take an interest in *[Expression] (to become interested in something)*.

He took an interest in politics and education.

She takes an interest in herself, and can make interesting to her students.

Drop in *[Verb] (to visit someone).*

My uncle dropped in at my house yesterday.

He dropped in on me last week.

Hang out *[Verb] (to spend a lot of time with someone in a place).*

My kids like to hang out at the mall.

We used to hang out at the pool.

Take it easy *[Verb] (to rest or relax).*

The doctor told him to take it easy for a while until he felt better.

We take it easy when we are tired.

Take it easy. Don't work so hard.

Intriguing *[Adjective] (very interesting; fascinating).*

I love this book. It is intriguing.

Make sure the introduction of your essay is intriguing and inviting.

To one's liking *[Expression] (to someone's taste (how somebody likes something)).*

Is the coffee to your liking?

It is to my liking to have at least a cup of tea every morning.

Put off *[Verb] (to delay doing something).*

The meeting has been put off until next week.

Never put off until tomorrow what you can do today.

Get into the habit of *[Expression] (to begin to do something regularly or often).*

He got into the habit of smoking and drinking soon after he quit his job.

She's got into the habit of biting her nails when she's nervous.

Give up *[Verb] (to quit or stop doing something).*

He is trying to give up drinking alcohol.

The doctor asked him to give up smoking.

Have a good command of *[Verb] (to have the ability to use something, especially a language).*

She's studied in Japan and has a good command of Japanese.

He has a good command of French.

Do a good deed *[Verb] (the action of doing a good thing).*

Helping someone or doing a good deed makes me feel good.

He thought he was doing a good deed when he saved her.

On a regular basis *[Expression] (regularly).*

I check my car on a regular basis to make sure that it is properly tuned.

My daughter drinks milk on a regular basis, every night.

Go sightseeing *[Verb] (to look around the places of interest).*

We are planning to go sightseeing in Rome next week.

Some of my friends like to lie on the beach, but I prefer to go sightseeing.

Be passionate about *[Expression] (really enjoy (doing) something).*

He is passionate about collecting stamps.

She is passionate about creating a culture of happiness.

Stay up late *[Expression] (to go to bed later than normal bedtime).*

I used to stay up late with my parents and watch TV.

My brother used to stay up late when he was a high school student.

Keep up with *[Expression]* *(to be able to continue to do something as planned)*.

He is struggling to keep up with the mortgage repayments.

He had a difficult time keeping up with all of the homework that his teacher gave him.

Pursue a goal *[Verb]* *(to follow something that someone wants to accomplish or achieve)*.

He kept pursuing his goal and didn't quit.

Susan was pursuing her goal to be a doctor.

Share a common interest *[Verb]* *(used to describe two or more people who enjoy doing similar things)*.

We share a common interest in photography.

He and I share a common interest in sports, and music.

For ages *[Adverb]* *(for a very long time)*.

I haven't seen her for ages.

I've been working at this job for ages.

On a daily basis *[Adverb]* *(every day)*.

I go swimming on a daily basis.

We eat on a daily basis.

Be more likely to *[Expression]* *(has a higher chance)*.

They will be more likely to buy from you again.

Customers will be more likely to choose the more expensive of the other two options.

Get into the habit of *[Expression]* *(make it a habit)*.

You ought to get into the habit of brushing your teeth before going to bed.

I get into the habit of drinking a glass of water every hour.

Get accustomed to *[Expression] (get used to; get familiar with).*

I've got accustomed to getting up so early.

You should try to get accustomed to the new working conditions as soon as possible.

To embark on *[Verb] (to start to do something).*

She embarked on her marriage with many hopes and fears.

We embarked on our trip to America with high hopes.

Take advantage of *[Expression] (use, take chance to use something).*

We took advantage of the fine weather to play football.

At the party, he took advantage of the chance to meet new people.

When it comes to *[Expression] (when talking about).*

When it comes to traffic there are no delays at the moment.

What is acceptable when it comes to air pollution?

Routine *[Noun] (a number of actions someone normally does as a habit).*

She is getting tired of the daily routine.

His job will be easier once he settles into a routine.

Regular *[Adverb] (usual; normal).*

Exercise has become a regular part of my lifestyle.

We made regular use of the car.

Every so often *[Adverb] (sometimes; from time to time; occasionally).*

He still phones me every so often.

I meet him at the club every so often.

Once in a blue moon *[Adverb] (very rarely; not very often).*

I used to spend a lot of time in Sydney, but now I only go there once in a blue moon.

My son lives in Italy and he only comes to see us once in a blue moon.

Used to *[Adverb] (to show that something is usually done or experienced in the past).*

I used to go swimming every day.

Tom used to exercise every morning, but since he had that terrible accident he doesn't exercise anymore.

All year round *[Adverb] (throughout the entire year).*

They had to work all year round.

I live here all year round now.

Adventurous *[Adjective] (willing to take risks and try new methods, or experiences).*

Our cat is not very adventurous, so she rarely goes outside.

Adam is an adventurous young man.

Have a whale of time *[Adverb] (have a good time).*

We all had a whale of time at the party.

I went to London when I was 22 and I had a whale of time.

Absorbed in *[Adjective] (to be very interested in something and do not notice anything else).*

He was completely absorbed in his work.

She was absorbed in the book.

Pleasurable *[Adjective] (enjoyable; pleasant).*

Eating out can be a very pleasurable experience.

This silk shirt feels very pleasurable on my skin.

In favor of *[Expression] (to support or approve of something).*

We are not in favor of hitting children.

He is in favor of stopping work.

Lost the habit *[Verb] (stopped an activity that you used to do often).*

I lost the habit of writing with hand after having got used to keyboard.

Most of us have lost the habit of reading newspapers.

Laziness *[Noun] (the quality of being unwilling to be active (do not want to work or make any effort)).*

The primary cause of Tom's failure is his laziness.

We scolded her for her laziness.

Enjoyable *[Adjective] (giving delight or pleasure).*

We had a most enjoyable evening.

Life is fine and enjoyable.

The teacher always tries to make her lessons enjoyable.

Amusement park = a theme park = funfair *[Noun] (an outdoor area for entertainment where people pay money to go on rides and play games to win prizes).*

The kids had a good time at the amusement park.

There's an amusement park planned on the grounds.

She likes pink cotton candy in an amusement park.

Slot machine *[Noun] (a machine that you put coins into to play gambling games).*

His coins all slotted into the slot machine.

My daughter really loved the sound of dice and slot machines.

Roller coaster *[Noun]* *(a structure like a tall railway with steep slopes that goes up and down at a high speed).*

She screamed herself silly on the roller coaster.

Mary means that her life is actually a real-life roller-coaster.

I have gone on the roller coaster three times and not be sick.

Pottery *[Noun]* *(vase, pots, cups, plates etc. that are made out of clay and baked in an oven).*

This pottery is made by a local artist.

People in England made pottery centuries ago.

Knitting *[Noun]* *(the activity of knitting things, such as sweaters, gloves, scarves etc).*

She loves knitting and working with fabrics.

She spent many days knitting a sweater for him.

To mow the lawn *[Verb]* *(to cut down (grass, grain, etc.) with a lawnmower).*

I want him to mow the lawn right after breakfast.

It's time to mow the lawn again.

I mow the lawn every week in summer.

THE MEDIA

Episode *[Noun] (a separate part of shows or television series).*

Each episode of that TV drama ends with somebody delivering a profound line.

I have watched every episode of the series he has appeared in.

Mass media *[Noun] (newspapers, magazines, television, radio, and the Internet).*

Students will be able to list several mass media.

I never trust the mass media.

Online scams = Internet fraud *[Noun] (a type of fraud performed by a dishonest individual, group who makes use of the Internet in order to make money).*

Protect yourself from online scams.

Nowadays, there are a variety of online scams, this includes obtaining money with fake photos, fake names, fake e-mails, etc.

Breaking news *[Noun] (newly received information about an event that is currently happening).*

The proportion of users who say they follow breaking news on Twitter is nearly twice as high as those who do so on Facebook.

My father tends to keep up with the latest breaking news around the world.

Commercial advertising *[Noun] (advertising on the radio or television, between or during programmes that is typically for the purpose of educating consumers or promoting specific product or service).*

Commercial advertising usually involves selling a product or service.

Many products promoted by commercial advertising are harmful to people's health and social relationships, as well as to the environment.

Live broadcast *[Noun]* *(live programmes on television or radio).*

We watched a live broadcast of the concert.

Is that a live broadcast of the event?

Classified ads *[Noun]* *(a short advertisement that you put in a newspaper or magazine, usually because you want to sell something).*

Classified ads can either be normal classified texts or classified display ads.

Unfortunately, too many people misuse classified ads.

Periodical *[Adjective]* *(a magazine or newspaper on a particular subject that is published regularly).*

She made periodical visits to her dentist.

A periodical town newsletter that is supported by local advertisers.

Domestic news *[Noun]* *(information about something that has happened recently of or inside a particular country).*

The newspaper provides more international news than domestic news.

International news

He usually updates the latest international news and world events from Asia, Europe, the Middle East, and more.

To keep abreast of something *[Expression]* *(to stay up-to-date with the new information about something).*

I often read the newspapers to keep abreast of current affairs.

We must keep abreast of the latest development in this field.

Entertaining *[Adjective]* *(amusing, funny and enjoyable).*

This TV program seems to be very entertaining.

The puppies are very entertaining.

Informative *[Adjective] (providing a lot of useful or interesting information).*

I read a very informative newspaper article this morning.

This site is very informative and helpful.

Publication *[Noun] (the process of producing a book, magazine, journal, piece of music, etc for public sale).*

Publication of the book was timed to coincide with the author's birthday.

Our company specializes in the publication of dictionaries.

BOOKS AND FILMS

Moviegoer *[Noun]* *(someone who regularly goes to the cinema).*

The film made America's moviegoers extremely excited.

Most moviegoers like to bring their own snacks to save money.

Sci-fi = science fiction *[Noun]* *(a form of fiction based on imagined future science).*

What is your favorite Sci-fi movie?

The Sci-fi films are more and more popular among young people.

Trailer *[Noun]* *(a series of short scenes from a film or television programme that shows in advance as its advertisement).*

The exciting trailer of the movie motivated him to watch the movie instead of studying for an exam.

Peter decided to go to see the movie after watching its exciting trailer.

Plot *[Noun]* *(the events which form the story of a book, film, play, etc).*

The film's plot is predictable and the acting is mediocre.

The book's plot revolves around a man who is searching for his missing daughter.

Spectacular *[Adjective]* *(amazing, fantastic, impressive or very exciting to look at).*

The view is spectacular and the atmosphere is absolutely unique.

The student who just left my class wrote a letter that is spectacular.

Suitable for *[Adjective]* *(right or appropriate for a particular purpose, someone or situation).*

The movie is not suitable for children.

A factory is not suitable for a residential district.

This material is not suitable for a dress.

Venue *[Noun]* *(the place where a concert, conference, or sports event is going to take place).*

The coffee house is a great venue for dining and team building activities.

Gig *[Noun]* *(a single performance by a musician, band or singer).*

Do you want to come with me to his gig?

It was a great gig.

Sitcom *[Noun]* *(a situation comedy with plots based on particular humorous situations).*

We couldn't stop laughing while watching a sitcom.

In my free time, I love watching a sitcom with my children.

Cinemagoer = moviegoer *[Noun]* *(a person who regularly goes to the cinema to watch films).*

The film put America's moviegoers into a feeding frenzy.

As a frequent cinemagoer, he is keeping abreast of the latest development of Hollywood movies.

Fascinating *[Adjective]* *(very interesting).*

Last night, I was reading a fascinating book called The History of Superstitions while I was waiting for him.

It really was a fascinating film.

(To) come highly recommended *[Expression]* *(to be praised by a lot of people).*

Breastfeeding has always come highly recommended due to great benefits it offers your baby.

Books by classic authors always come highly recommended.

(To) stick in one's mind *[Expression] (a memory or image which is remembered clearly and for a long time).*

He says numbers just stick in his mind!

Those judgments stick in his mind and influence his attitudes.

Keep one's eyes glued to screens *[Expression] (to watch (something) in a very concentrated way for a long time).*

When people keep their eyes glued to screens for several hours, waves from computers and wifi devices may cause headaches.

He kept his eyes glued to the screen.

Security guards have to keep their eyes glued to screens of security cameras to look for criminals entering the building.

Frustrated *[Adjective] (feeling annoyed, disappointed or dissatisfied because you cannot achieve what you want).*

They felt frustrated at the lack of progress.

He had a disagreement with his partner and felt frustrated.

(To) grasp *[Verb] (to comprehend/understand something completely).*

He was able to grasp everything I taught in this lesson.

The talk was interesting, but as the topic was new to me, I did not grasp everything that the speaker told us.

By leaps and bounds *[Expression] (very quickly).*

His Japanese is improving by leaps and bounds.

Curious *[Adjective] (having a strong desire to know or learn something).*

The neighbors very curious about our business.

We are very curious about where the animals came from.

Enthralling *[Adjective] (capturing someone's full interest and attention).*

I found his book absolutely enthralling!

Your idea is absolutely enthralling!

Broaden one's knowledge *[Verb] (to widen one's knowledge of something).*

He is taking some courses to broaden his knowledge.

She took advantage of her father's extensive library to broaden her knowledge.

Reference book *[Noun] (a book that is intended to be used for information on specific matters, for example, a dictionary, encyclopedia, atlas etc).*

A dictionary is an excellent reference book.

It is a very thorough grammar reference book with clear explanations.

Bedtime story *[Noun] (a story read or told to children at bedtime).*

My mother used to read me bedtime stories.

My dad read me a bedtime story every night.

Blockbuster *[Noun] (a book, show or film that is very successful).*

That new movie is a blockbuster.

That blockbuster made about 40 million dollars.

Action movie = Kung Fu film *[Noun] (a film/movie that contains lots of action and violence).*

Jack has loved action movies since he was a teenager.

Action movies and horror films are my favourite genres.

Animated film *[Noun] (cartoon).*

A new live-action version of the classic animated film will be released later this year.

After dinner, he likes watching animated film.

Horror films *[Noun]* *(a film with a frightening storyline and atmosphere, especially the one about murders, frightening creatures, or evil people).*

Do you enjoy watching horror films?

I don't like horror movies.

Release *[Verb]* *(to set free).*

When will the film be released?

The movie will be released next month.

Subtitle *[Noun]* *(a translation displayed at the bottom of a movie screen).*

A secondary or explanatory title.

The film is in Chinese with English subtitles.

A feast for the eyes and ears *[Noun]* *(to describe something that is pleasant to watch and listen to).*

The movie truly was a feast for the eyes and ears.

Seeing The Focke Wolves perform for the first time was a feast for the eyes and ears.

Censorship *[Noun]* *(the act of supervising).*

The library used censorship to keep some books off their shelves.

They applied censorship to all radio stations in the country.

Poetic *[Adjective]* *(connected with poetry).*

The piece ends with a truly poetic slow movement.

The lyrics to some of the Beatles' songs were often quite poetic.

The description of the city is quite poetic and romantic.

Action-packed *[Adjective]* *(full of exciting activities, events).*

TAKEN is one of the most action-packed movies I have ever watched!

My brother loves big-budget, action-packed movies.

Addictive *[Adjective]* *(something is so enjoyable that you quickly become addicted to)*.

Video games can be quite addictive for young kids.

The TV show is very addictive.

Creepy *[Adjective]* *(producing a feeling of fear, scary or unease)*.

The house looked OK from the outside but inside it was all dark and creepy.

It feels a bit creepy in here.

There's something creepy about the building.

Dreary *[Adjective]* *(sad, boring or depressing)*.

After the death of her grandmother, she was in a dreary mood for weeks.

The song was dreary and repetitive.

Heartbreaking *[Adjective]* *(making you feel extremely sad or upset)*.

It is heartbreaking that she cannot see her children.

It was a heartbreaking story.

Inspirational *[Adjective]* *(making you feel enthusiastic or encouraged to do something)*.

Last week, I read a very inspirational book called The Power of Now.

In my mind, he is a very inspirational author because he shows us many things that we can do.

The quotes are very inspirational.

Tear-jerking *[Adjective]* *(sad, tragic, making you cry)*.

The film Annie is a tear-jerking story about an orphan.

The movie is very romantic and very tear-jerking.

Box office hit *[Noun]* *(a very successful movie that a lot of tickets are well sold).*

Her last film was a surprise box-office hit.

The movie became a box-office record breaker.

E-reader *[Noun]* *(a portable electronic device on which you can read books, newspapers, magazines, etc).*

I want to read my books on my e-reader, not on my computer.

She actually goes to the library more than she did before she had her e-reader.

From cover to cover *[Expression]* *(from the beginning to the end (a book or magazine)).*

It's a book to be read from cover to cover.

I read the newspaper from cover to cover on the train.

Hardcover *[Noun]* *(a book that has a hardcover (bound in cloth, leather)).*

Her friend gave her a hardcover book as a present for her birthday.

The novel was published in hardcover.

Page turner *[Noun]* *(a book that is very interesting or exciting that you want to read it quickly).*

The book is a page-turner and now I cannot take a break until I complete reading it.

Even though we know the outcome, the story is a page-turner.

The book so interesting that she can't stop reading. It is a page turner.

Don't judge a book by its cover *[Expression]* *(you shouldn't judge someone or something only from their appearance).*

That woman may look very slow and awkward, but don't judge a book by its cover. She is a very intelligent woman in her circle.

I know I look serious in my picture, hope you don't judge a book by its cover.

To catch the latest movie *[Verb]* *(to see a film that has just come out).*

I am going to grab a pizza and catch the latest movie with my friends at the theatre.

PVR Cinemas is the ideal place to catch the latest movie.

To flick through *[Verb]* *(to look through a book quickly).*

She flicked through her diary, looking for the appointed date.

He flicked through the book and found the photo.

To know like a book *[Verb]* *(to know someone or something extremely well).*

I know him like a book.

He lives in this city for his whole life and he knows it like a book.

URBANISATION

Hometown *[Noun] (the city or town where you were born or grew up).*

I am planning to go to my hometown this weekend.

My hometown is located about 10 kilometers from a large city.

Born and raised in *[Expression] (someone was born in a certain place grew up there with his/her parents).*

I was born and raised in Sydney but moved to New York when I was 25.

She was born and raised in London.

Rustic *[Adjective] (simple, old-fashioned and typical of the countryside; rural).*

The old temple in the small village had a rustic appearance.

The small rustic house is used as a temporary shelter.

Get stuck *[Verb] (to be unable to escape from or move further).*

I get stuck in traffic on the way to my office sometimes.

Sacred *[Adjective] (connected with a god, and considered to be holy).*

We are not allowed to use a mobile phone in the sacred temple.

Metropolitan *[Noun] (relating to/ connected with a large city).*

His family lives in the New York metropolitan area.

Commute *[Verb] (the journey between one's home and place of work).*

I saw him when I was commuting to the store.

Do you commute to school by bus?

Peak traffic hours *[Noun] (the time of day when traffic is at its heaviest).*

Taxis are difficult to catch on rainy days and during peak traffic hours.

Exercising in urban areas during peak traffic hours is unhealthy.

Horn [Noun] *(a device in a vehicle for making a loud noise as a warning).*

Honk [Verb] *(to make a loud noise like a warning sound).*

Tom honked his horn at the kids playing in the street.

Can't you hear all the car horns honking behind us?

Diverse [Adjective] *(a wide range of people or things).*

Sydney is a large city with people from diverse backgrounds.

It's quite challenging to work with children and families from diverse cultures.

Heavy traffic congestion [Noun] *(the state of having so many vehicles or people that it is difficult to move around).*

Heavy traffic congestion usually takes place on the roads in the morning.

Tom always blames the heavy traffic congestion when he is late for work.

Slow down [Verb] *(to move more slowly).*

The road is quite bumpy, so you should slow down a bit.

You are driving too fast - just slow down a bit.

Chaotic [Adjective] *(completely confused or disordered).*

The traffic in the city is chaotic during the rush hour.

World-famous [Adjective] *(known or famous throughout the world).*

Titanic a world-famous film.

Harvard is a world-famous university.

He is a world-famous specialist on/in geology.

Outskirts *[Adverb]* *(the part of a town or city that is far away from its center).*

She lives a three-bedroom apartment on the outskirts of Paris.

Our new factory is on the outskirts of New Delhi.

The rush hour *[Noun]* *(a time during each day when the roads are full of traffic).*

Traffic is very heavy during the rush hour.

I can't stand traveling in the rush hour.

Municipal *[Adjective]* *(related to the city).*

The city is planning to build a municipal library.

His father is a municipal judge.

Traffic jam *[Noun]* *(a situation in which a lot of vehicles are very close together so that they cannot move forward).*

I was stuck in a traffic jam for two hours this morning.

There is a traffic jam on the highway.

He was stuck in a traffic jam while he was driving home.

Facilities *[Noun]* *(buildings, pieces of equipment, or services provided at a certain place for a particular purpose).*

The town has excellent sports facilities.

The resort has a wide range of facilities for young people.

Eatery *[Noun]* *(a small place where people can buy and eat food).*

How much is a lunch in a cheap eatery?

There's a good cheap eatery a few doors down.

Crowded *[Adjective]* *(to be full of people or things).*

The road was crowded with various vehicles.

This room is too crowded with many people in it.

Modernise *[Verb] (to make something more modern).*

We're modernizing our kitchen with a new refrigerator, oven, and dishwasher.

Architecture *[Noun] (the character or design style of buildings and similar structures).*

The architecture of that building was fantastic.

Competitive *[Adjective] (having a strong desire to win or do better than other people).*

Since he is very competitive, I know he will try and surpass my video game score.

He is very competitive, he sometimes puts too much pressure on himself.

Challenging *[Adjective] (used to describe something that is difficult and intriguing).*

Nursing is a very challenging and demanding career.

I found this to be very challenging.

Dweller *[Noun] (a person who lives in a particular city, town, etc).*

Many urban dwellers are homeless or live in inadequate housing.

Urban dwellers often accept noise as part of city life.

Outlet *[Noun] (a place that sells goods).*

She bought her clothes at an outlet mall.

The outlet store will be closing after 11 pm.

Metropolis *[Noun] (a very large city, often the capital city of a country).*

A modern metropolis needs a good integrated transport system.

Many young people like to live in a modern metropolis.

A metropolis is never silent.

Hustle and bustle *[Expression]* *(busy and noisy, involving a lot of activities and work)*.

We can't concentrate on our lessons with all the hustle and bustle going on around us.

Last week, I moved to my parents' farm to stay away from the hustle and bustle of the city life.

Renovation *[Noun]* *(the process of repairing and improving a building to restore to good condition)*.

The temple is in bad need of renovation.

The restaurant was closed due to its renovation.

The lungs of the city *[Noun]* *(places in the city where the air is less polluted)*.

The parks and green infrastructure of our city are the lungs of the city.

The parklands are the lungs of the city since they purify much of the air pollution.

Overcrowded *[Adjective]* *(to be excessively crowded (with too many people or things in a place)*.

The county jail is overcrowded.

Too many poor people are living in overcrowded conditions.

A passer-by *[Noun]* *(a person who is walking past you (in the street))*.

By a fortunate coincidence, a passer-by heard her cries for help.

He was rescued by a passer-by.

Modes of transport = means of transport *[Noun]* *(particular types of transport)*.

The line graph shows three modes of transport used by people living in London.

He likes to use his bicycle because it is an environmentally-friendly mode of transport.

Residential areas *[Noun] (places with private houses in which people live).*

Housing may vary significantly between, and through, residential areas.

He lives in one of the residential areas of the city, far from all the factories and offices.

Retirement home *[Noun] (a house in which old people live and are cared for by staff).*

My parents now live in a retirement home.

When she was 75, my aunt went into a retirement home.

Sanitation *[Noun] (the process of keeping places clean and healthy).*

Many countries over the world suffer from diseases due to a lack of sanitation systems.

A lack of clean water and sanitation are the main causes of life-threatening diseases.

There was a proper sanitation in the hospital.

Emigration *[Noun] (the act of leaving your own country to go and live permanently in another country; moving abroad).*

The emigration of birds from cold climates to warmer ones is fascinating to me.

Emigration from Ireland increased after a widespread famine.

Overconsumption *[Noun] (excessive consumption (the act of consuming something to excess)).*

The overconsumption of alcohol can damage health, both in the short term and long term.

Overconsumption of fat and sugar is a leading cause of obesity.

Exploitation *[Noun] (the use of something (land, oil or other natural resources) in* *order to get an advantage or profit from it).*

Commercial exploitation of resources threatens our survival.

The exploitation of recycled materials can only be beneficial to our pollution problems.

Safeguard *[Verb] (to protect something or someone from harm or damage).*

The boss explained how the employees should safeguard themselves while at work.

The industry has a duty to safeguard the interests of consumers.

Mitigate *[Verb] (to make something less harmful, unpleasant, severe, or serious).*

The doctor gave me a prescription to mitigate the pain.

To mitigate the problem of homelessness, the government is building more places for poor people to stay.

Inflated *[Adjective] ((prices, costs, numbers, etc.) are excessively or unreasonably high).*

The houses were sold at inflated prices, so few people could afford to buy them.

They had to buy everything at inflated prices at the ranch store.

Living standards *[Noun] (the amount of money and level of comfort that people have in a particular society).*

Living standards have improved over the last century.

Cheaper housing would vastly improve the living standards of ordinary people.

The hectic pace of life *[Noun] (a life that is almost always very busy or chaotic).*

The hectic pace of life suddenly slows down.

Today's hectic pace of life encourages fast food and hasty meals.

The increasingly hectic pace of life has also increased interest in silence and tranquility.

Downtown *[Adverb] (the centre of main business or shopping area of a town or city).*

The skyscraper is in the downtown.

I have walked downtown many times before.

We used to go to the bars downtown, but more recently we've been hanging out in the suburbs.

Block of flats *[Noun] (a large building that consists of many apartments).*

It took us ages to get used to living in a block of flats.

They lived in a block of flats.

Upmarket *[Adjective] (services or goods are designed for people who are rich).*

Japanese firms have moved steadily upmarket.

I felt truly welcome for such an upmarket restaurant.

Posh *[Adjective] (luxurious, fashionable, expensive and attractive).*

Her posh bag was very expensive.

His posh yacht was a very lavish boat used for traveling to vacation destinations.

Luxurious *[Adjective] (very expensive, elegant and comfortable).*

This is a luxurious car complete with air conditioning.

They spent their honeymoon in a luxurious motel at Long Beach.

Sumptuous *[Adjective] (splendid, expensive, and of high quality).*

The jewellery which were robbed were very sumptuous.

Her boyfriend treated her to a sumptuous meal for her birthday.

We had a very sumptuous dinner in the jungle.

Opulent *[Adjective]* *(expensive and luxurious; very impressive).*

Most of the cash went on supporting his opulent lifestyle.

He lived in an opulent mansion with many antiques and relics.

Stressful *[Adjective]* *(making someone worried and nervous).*

Her job's getting more and more stressful.

Being a manager can be stressful.

The business environment can be stressful.

Bustling *[Adjective]* *(to be full of noise and activity).*

It is a bustling shopping mall.

She is bustling about in the kitchen.

The street was bustling with shoppers.

Nursing home *[Noun]* *(an institution where old people live to receive medical treatment and care).*

His family put him into a nursing home.

Her mother lives in a nursing home.

Medical care *[Noun]* *(health care provided by a medical professional).*

For the homeless, private medical care is simple.

The children have inadequate medical care and little formal education.

If she gets proper medical care, she will survive.

Divorce rate *[Noun]* *(the ratio between the number of divorces).*

The divorce rate is expected to rise.

The divorce rate has actually been decreasing for decades.

ENVIRONMENT, WEATHER, CLIMATE CHANGE AND POLLUTION

Rubbish *[Noun] (trash, garbage, waste material).*

The streets were littered with rubbish.

There is too much rubbish in this yard. Let's clean it up!

Littering *[Noun] (to drop trash on the ground rather than put it in the trash bin).*

Littering is prohibited.

People destroy the beauty of the beach through littering.

Unsorted *[Verb] (not categorized or sorted).*

Most of the shirts were unsorted, so all the colors were mixed together.

The data were unsorted.

Diminish *[Verb] (to go down; to lessen).*

After he took the aspirin, the pain was diminished.

Our sugar supplies are diminished.

To throw something out *[Verb] (to get rid of something).*

He has thrown out his old boots.

Waste treatment *[Noun] (the treatment of materials that are no longer used).*

Alternative waste treatment technologies.

Cleaner technologies in waste treatment and recycling.

Impact *[Noun] (an effect or influence of something on something else).*

The impact of the storm has yet to be fully understood.

The bad weather had a significant impact on our profits.

Freshen *[Verb] (to make something newer, cleaner, cooler and more pleasant).*

The rain freshened the air.

We freshened up the apartment by making new curtains.

Sparkle *[Verb] (to shine brightly with flashes of light).*

The sky sparkled with brilliant stars.

The moonlit air sparkled with frost.

The air sparkled with freshness.

Drizzle *[Noun] (light rain and falling steadily in fine drops).*

The drizzle was so light that she didn't need an umbrella.

Would you like to go for a walk in the drizzle?

Pollution *[Noun] (the act of polluting air or water).*

Air pollution is a serious health hazard.

The highest level of water pollution is caused by the high use of fertilizers, insecticides, and pesticides.

Clear sky *[Noun] (a sky that is bright and clear).*

The forecast was for a clear sky this morning.

Throw something out *[Verb] (to discard or get rid of something).*

She threw out all her old clothes to make some space in her wardrobe.

I threw out all my son's old comics.

Get rid of *[Verb] (to remove; to abolish).*

We'll get rid of this old furniture.

It's time to get rid of this old sweater.

It is difficult to get rid of insects.

Eco-friendly *[Adjective] (not or less harmful or damaging to the environment).*

The government encourage people to use eco-friendly products or services.

For environmentally conscious people, it is very easy to use eco-friendly products and organic food.

Emit *[Verb] (to produce and discharge something, like gases or radiation for example).*

When the volcano exploded, it emitted clouds of gases and smoke into the air.

It is predicted that trucks will produce about 23 tons of CO2 and vans will emit 15 tons.

Global warming *[Noun] (the gradual increase in temperature of the atmosphere of the Earth caused by high levels of carbon dioxide and other gases in the atmosphere).*

Greater use of renewable energy resources is necessary in order to combat global warming.

Global warming has become a real problem for the earth.

In all weathers *[Expression] (if something is done in all weathers, it is done whether the weather is good or bad).*

He goes out jogging in all weathers.

We go fishing in all weathers.

To be spoiled by *[Verb] (to be ruined by).*

The football match was spoiled by the wind and the rain.

Our camping trip was spoiled by bad weather.

Minimize *[Verb] (to reduce something (especially something unpleasant) to the lowest possible level or amount).*

If you obey the rules of the road, you can minimize the dangers of your driving.

We ought to install a good alarm system in order to minimize the risk of burglary.

The risk of infections could be minimized if conditions in hospitals are clean.

Contamination *[Noun] (the act of polluting or poisoning a place by adding a substance that is dangerous).*

People are suffering from the contamination of the water supply.

New-born babies must be isolated from possible contamination.

Devastates *[Verb] (to completely destroy or ruin (a place or thing)).*

An entire town was devastated by an earthquake.

A hurricane devastated the state, flooding many coastal towns and left thousands homeless.

Eliminate *[Verb] (to remove or get rid of something, especially something you do not want or need).*

She's trying to eliminate fatty foods from her diet.

The company plans to eliminate more than 500 jobs in the coming year.

Gloomy *[Adjective]* **(dark or dim; feeling sad and without hope).**

The gloomy weather shows no sign of improving.

He looks gloomy.

The sky was dark and gloomy.

Freezing = chilly *[Adjective] (very cold).*

The temperature remained below freezing point throughout the day.

The air temperature was well below freezing.

It's freezing outside!

Boiling hot *[Adjective] ((of weather) very hot))*.

The sun was boiling hot, the average temperature reached 42 degrees!

The soup is boiling hot when poured into a bowl.

Mild *[Adjective] ((of weather) warm and pleasant)*.

The weather in my country is mild but damp.

I think it's terrific because the climate is mild.

Chilly *[Adjective] (unpleasantly cold)*.

In spite of the sunny weather, the air was rather chilly.

The bathroom gets chilly in the winter.

It's chilly today, so I think you should wear a coat.

Degrees Celsius *[Noun] (a temperature scale (used to measure the temperature))*.

Water boils at 100 degrees Celsius.

Temperatures vary between 8 and 20 degrees Celsius.

To go below zero *[Verb] (to become negative (about temperatures))*.

The temperature often goes below zero degrees in January, February, and March.

Cloudy weather *[Noun] ((of the sky or weather) covered with a lot of clouds)*.

The forecast is for dry, cloudy weather with no precipitation expected.

I dislike cloudy weather.

Rainy weather *[Noun] ((of the weather) to rain a lot)*.

I never go to the park in rainy weather.

We went to the beach in spite of the rainy weather.

To be drenched (to the skin) *[Adjective] (to be completely wet).*

I was caught in a shower and was drenched to the skin.

He was drenched while it was going to rain.

John was drenched by the rain and frozen by the icy wind.

Downpour *[Noun] (a heavy rain).*

The heavy downpour brought their picnic to an abrupt end.

The air was still fresh following a downpour the day before.

The downpour and the resultant flood destroyed almost every house.

To pour down *[Verb] (to rain heavily).*

The air is warm, but rain pours down constantly.

It has been pouring down since two o'clock.

Humid *[Adjective] (hot and wet in a way that makes us feel uncomfortable).*

The recent hot, humid weather is affecting air quality.

If it is hot and humid, then it is raining.

Heavy snow *[Noun] (when a lot of snow falls).*

He came in spite of the heavy snow.

In spite of heavy snow and cold temperatures, the game continued.

Heavy snow continues to fall at the airport.

Snowstorm *[Noun] (a large amount of snow).*

It had been delayed by several days due to a snowstorm in the area.

All the schools were closed since there was a big snowstorm.

Windy weather *[Noun] ((of the weather) with a lot of wind).*

I can fly my kite in windy weather.

The flower does not bloom well in windy weather.

Sunny weather *[Noun]* *((of the weather) with a lot of bright light from the sun).*

We are having sunny weather today.

In spite of the sunny weather, the air was rather chilly.

They wanted sunny weather for an enjoyable picnic.

Sunshine *[Noun]* *(the shining or direct light of the sun).*

I love summertime because of the long days and bright sunshine.

Despite the sunshine, the snow has not yet melted.

This is the only day we've had sunshine all week.

Changeable weather *[Noun]* *(weather that tends to change suddenly and often).*

The heavy rain might settle the changeable weather.

The accident was caused chiefly by the changeable weather.

Mild climate *[Noun]* *(a climate with pleasant conditions).*

Japan has a mild climate.

The mild climate lets us enjoy outdoor activities like running, and playing volleyball all year round.

Endangered species *[Noun]* *(a type of animal or plant that might become extinct).*

The giant panda is an endangered species.

Endangered species are those considered to be at risk of extinction.

Environmentally friendly *[Noun]* *(not harmful to the environment).*

Environmentally friendly materials are used to minimize pollution.

The most important quality of bamboo is its environmentally friendly quality.

Exhaust fumes *[Noun] (gases, ejected from an engine that is unpleasant, and sometimes dangerous).*

Exhaust fumes from cars are poisoning the air of our cities.

The air was heavily polluted with exhaust fumes.

Fossil fuels *[Noun] (energy resources like gas, coal and oil).*

There are three major types of fossil fuels: coal, natural gas, and oil.

Most of the fuels people burn are fossil fuels.

Global warming *[Noun] (an increase in the amount of carbon dioxide in the atmosphere all-over the world, as a result of greenhouse effect).*

The cause of global warming occurs because of greenhouse gases.

Global warming is a very serious problem that our society is dealing with.

Greenhouse effect *[Noun] (the rise in temperature of the atmosphere due to the carbon dioxide and other gases).*

Greenhouse effect causes global warming.

Earth would be too cold for life to exist without the greenhouse effect.

Natural disaster *[Noun] (a natural event such as a flood, earthquake, or hurricane that causes great damage or loss of life).*

Almost 15,000 people were killed in the natural disaster.

The flood in 1995 was the worst natural disaster in our country.

Toxic waste *[Noun] (industrial or chemical waste materials that are harmful to living things and the environment).*

The company was fined $6.5 million for dumping toxic waste into the river.

Toxic wastes were detected in the water samples.

To become extinct *[Adjective] (to stop existing (not now existing)).*

Unless whales are protected, they will become extinct.

Plant and animal species become extinct for many reasons, including climate change, disease, etc.

To be under threat *[Expression] (likely to be harmed, damaged or become extinct).*

The house was under threat of demolition.

She lives daily under threat of violence.

To get back to nature *[Expression] (to start living a more simple life that is closer to nature).*

We went on a camping trip to get back to nature.

There are plenty of ways to get back to nature, even if you live in a city.

Biodiversity *[Noun] (a diversity of plants and animals in a particular region).*

The newcomers can pose a threat to biodiversity by altering ecosystems.

Biodiversity continues to decline each year.

Contaminated *[Adjective] (made dirty, polluted, or poisonous by adding something that is dangerous or carries a disease).*

He died because he had eaten some contaminated beef.

Many bays and coastal waters have been contaminated with heavy metals.

Deforestation *[Noun] (the action of cutting down of a wide area of trees).*

Deforestation is destroying large areas of tropical rainforest.

Their habitat is threatened by deforestation.

Ecosystems *[Noun] (all the animals and plants that live in a particular area).*

Dynamite fishing is extremely destructive to reef ecosystems.

What efforts have been increased to save our ecosystems?

Exhaust emissions *[Noun] (waste gases that are released from a vehicle and go into the air)*.

Car manufacturers must cut down the exhaust emissions that cause smog.

The reduction of exhaust emissions from diesel engines.

Contaminate *[Verb] (make a place or something dirty or poisonous by adding a chemical, waste, or infection)*.

To contaminate a lake with sewage.

Industrial chemicals contaminate the atmosphere.

Discharge *[Verb] (to release gas, liquid, or other harmful substances into the water or the air)*.

The chemical company was fined for discharging chemicals into the river.

Erosion *[Noun] (the action or process of eroding by wind, water, or other natural agents)*.

For many years, the town has been threatened by the erosion of the river banks.

Soil erosion was mitigated by the planting of trees.

Drought *[Noun] (a long period of time when there is little or no rain)*.

The area was constantly hit by drought.

The land ploughs hard after the drought.

Recycle *[Verb] (to convert waste materials such as newspapers and bottles into reusable material)*.

To reduce global warming, we should recycle paper and water bottles as often as we can.

Recycling cans and bottles are compulsory to town residents.

BUILDING, ACCOMMODATION, HOUSES, FLATS, AND ROOMS

Pagoda *[Noun]* *(a temple; a religious building/ a sacred building).*

There are three entrances to the pagoda.

Many people go to the pagoda to pray for a good year for themselves.

Skyrocketing *[Verb]* *(to increase rapidly).*

Skyrocketing hospital costs.

Skyrocketing costs of insurance have hurt small businesses.

Balcony *[Noun]* *(a small platform with a wall or rail around it for safety that is built on the outside wall of a building).*

The glass doors opened on to a balcony with a view of the river.

He led us to a room with a balcony overlooking the sea.

Corridor *[Noun]* *(a long passage inside a building that people walk along).*

The corridor was so crowded that we couldn't walk.

The corridor opens into his office.

Low- rise *[Adjective]* *(describing buildings which have few stories (just one or two stories)).*

Low-rise residential buildings.

Low-rise apartment buildings.

Cozy *[Adjective]* *(small, but comfortable, warm, relaxing and safe).*

My uncle's house was cozy and simple.

The room was cozy and pleasing to the eye.

Narrow *[Adjective]* *(limited in space (length, width)).*

A narrow part or passage.

The street is very narrow.

Apartment building *[Noun] (a large building that is divided into apartments).*

There's a nine-story apartment building next to the bank.

She recently cancelled her personal wifi and joined her apartment building's free wifi.

Elegant *[Adjective] (attractive, graceful and stylish in appearance or style).*

Yellow lights made the room seem warm and elegant.

He was so elegant in a suit.

She is so elegant that everybody admires her.

Cramped *[Adjective] (describing a place where there is not enough space for people or things in it).*

It was so cramped that it looked like a cupboard.

We can fit seven people in our tent, but it'll be very cramped.

Messy *[Adjective] (untidy, dirty, or badly organized).*

I couldn't endure that messy room.

His bedroom was so messy.

Cosy *[Adjective] (to be comfortable, warm, and relaxing).*

It was raining outside, but inside it was warm and very cosy.

My room is very cosy.

Scuffy *[Adjective] (untidy, messy).*

She always wears scruffy clothes.

He has black scruffy hair.

Homely *[Adjective]* *((of a place) simple but cozy, pleasant and comfortable).*

I loved my small but extremely homely room.

The main part of the hotel is extremely homely and there is a large terrace with a stunning view.

Run down *[Adjective]* *(to be in very bad condition).*

He bought a run-down television station.

The whole area's really run-down.

Pavilion *[Noun]* *(a beautiful building, used for a specific purpose, such as shelter, concerts, events, etc).*

I was attracted by the porcelain doll of Peony Pavilion.

The pavilion on the hill looks down on the river.

Chores *[Noun]* *(tasks such as cleaning, washing, and ironing that are often boring but has to be done regularly).*

Many husbands now help with the household chores like washing the dishes and cleaning the floor.

My neighbor's kids have to do chores every day in order to earn their allowance.

Upkeep *[Verb]* *(to look after/ keep something in good condition).*

The expenses of upkeeping the building are quite expensive.

Historical monument *[Noun]* *(ancient buildings, statues, or other structures that have historical importance).*

The historical monument is one most visited tourist attractions in Kuala Lumpur.

Overlooking the majestic Arabian Sea, this historical monument is located in a perfect scenic spot.

Chores *[Noun]* *(daily work of a household).*

I have some chores to do.

My neighbor's kids have to do chores every day in order to earn their allowance.

Construction site *[Noun] (an area of land where a building, etc, is built).*

Hard hats must be worn on the construction site.

The area is now full of machinery, because it is now the construction site for a new road.

International hotel *[Noun] (an international trade association providing lodging, meals, and other guest services on a short-term basis).*

My friend and I stayed in the International Hotel at the weekend and it was outstanding.

Installation *[Noun] (the action or process of installing something, so that it can be used).*

After the installation of solar panels on the roof of his house, his electricity bills were reduced.

The devices are usually tested before installation.

Majestic *[Adjective] (big, beautiful, powerful or impressive in admiration way).*

The majestic mountains were all around us.

His house is majestic in design.

Tatty *[Adjective] (old and in poor condition).*

His friends used to tease him about his tatty clothes.

The man wore a tatty and worn raincoat.

That book is tatty.

Dusty *[Adjective] (covered with dust).*

The trees were dusty and the rivers were dry.

It was a hot and dusty day.

The book on the shelf is very dusty.

Shabby *[Adjective]* *(old and in poor condition)*.

His first apartment was pretty shabby.

The furniture was old and shabby.

The old house has grown shabby with age.

Condo (short for condominium) *[Noun]* *(an apartment that someone owns in a building)*.

He lives in a high-rise condo.

They live on the 12th floor of this condo.

High-rise *[Adjective]* *(a very tall building with many floors or levels)*.

The city was overlooked by a ring of high-rise buildings.

My parents live in a high-rise flat.

Skyscraper *[Noun]* *(a very tall modern building of many floors for office or commercial use)*.

Skyscrapers are almost always found in big cities.

Many skyscrapers in the city were damaged in the hurricane.

Construction *[Noun]* *(the action of building something large or complicated)*.

The construction of the building will be started next year.

The bridge is still under construction.

TIME

Timely *[Adjective]* *(refers to something done or happening at the right time).*

You must make timely payments.

Their work is timely, accurate and cost-efficient.

Once in a lifetime *[Adverb]* *(a chance that is very rarely to happen to someone again in his/her life).*

This is a once-in-a-lifetime chance to earn thousands of dollars from home.

This is the once-in-a-lifetime chance to build my industry network and grow my career.

Annually *[Adverb]* *(once a year; yearly; every year).*

Parents are supposed to report annually how the money is used.

My brother loves to travel, he visits London annually.

How many cars do they produce annually?

The coming year *[Adverb]* *(the next year).*

I will celebrate my 30th birthday in February of the coming year.

In the coming years, it is anticipated that tourism will continue to develop in Asia.

Up to the minute *[Adverb]* *(very latest; the most recent).*

Her clothes are always right up to the minute.

The traffic reports are up to the minute.

A digital watch *[Noun]* *(a watch shows the hours, minutes, and sometimes seconds as a row of numbers).*

Your digital watch is quite nice.

My father bought me a digital watch as a birthday present.

Punctual *[Adverb] (on time; arriving or happening at the expected, correct time).*

She is always punctual, but her friend is always late.

He is a very punctual boy.

He likes his guests to be punctual.

Upcoming *[Adjective] (be about to happen; happening soon).*

Tom could use a little extra time to review for the upcoming test.

I used to study a lot when I had an upcoming exam.

Take your time *[Expression] (not hurry (to do something slowly or carefully)).*

Take your time. There's no hurry.

Take your time and read each sentence carefully.

He didn't like us to rush him, he wished to take his time over the work.

On time *[Adverb] (punctual; punctually (arriving at the correct time and not late)).*

She started on time, but she arrived late.

Students must attend class regularly and submit all of their homework on time.

Right after *[Adverb] (immediately after).*

He arrived right after me.

He quit his job right after he won the lottery ticket.

Lucy was hired by the company right after she graduated.

Nowadays *[Adverb] (these days; now; at the present time).*

Nowadays, it's easy to buy foreign products.

There is an increasing number of people who don't watch TV very much nowadays.

Age-old *[Adjective]* *(having existed for ages)*.

Giving much priority is age-old custom, but not in modern days.

Celebrating New Year with age-old traditions.

Going to pagodas during Lunar New Year is one of Asia's age-old traditions.

Down the road *[Adverb]* *(in the future)*.

It can be achieved down the road.

This deal will be beneficial down the road.

Right away *[Adverb]* *(immediately)*.

I have to go back right away.

He did not reply to my question right away.

Currently *[Adverb]* *(now; at the present time)*.

I currently do not make as much money as I used to.

My uncle is currently working for the government in the Department of Finance.

Time-consuming *[Adjective]* *(taking a lot of/ too much time)*.

It was a time-consuming process, but it was the only way the job could be done.

This is a very time-consuming task.

In this day and age *[Adverb]* *(at the present time)*.

In this day and age recording videos is easier than ever.

In this day and age, life without water and electricity is unimaginable.

Ancient *[Adjective]* *(very old).*

A king in ancient times had many slaves to work for him.

My parents live in a lovely, gigantic, ancient, brick house.

Brand-new *[Adjective]* *(extremely new).*

He bought himself a brand new car yesterday.

His waterproof trousers were brand new and stiff.

Antique *[Adjective]* *(ancient; very old).*

The fashion of carving animals as a device appears to have a very antique origin.

My grandfather has an antique watch that he wants to give me.

Middle-aged *[Adjective]* *(no longer young but not yet old; in middle age).*

The company is run almost entirely by middle-aged men.

They're a middle-aged couple, with grown-up children.

Her novels are middle-aged and boring.

Contemporary *[Adjective]* *(current, modern, nowadays; belonging to the present time).*

Young people tend to prefer contemporary music.

Traditional and contemporary fashion design.

Childhood *[Noun]* *(the period of your life when you are a child).*

He used to play with her in his childhood.

In the childhood, we used to play different types of games.

Quality time *[Noun]* *(time that you spend with only one person in order to strengthen a relationship).*

Her father didn't spend enough quality time with him. He always had to work.

Parents should spend quality time with their children.

TRAVEL, TOURISM & HOLIDAYS

Show someone around *[Verb] (to act as a guide for someone when they are visiting a new place or building and to show them what is interesting in such place or building).*

They were shown around the church by one of the local people.

I will show us around the city tomorrow.

Take place *[Verb] (to occur; to happen).*

Their wedding took place in London.

The graduation ceremony will take place tomorrow.

Scenery *[Noun] (beautiful nature scenes/landscapes).*

The scenery here is very beautiful.

The scenery of the Porvoo river valley is breathtaking.

Rays *[Noun] (narrow beams of light).*

The rays of the sun fell upon the trees.

The rays of the sun breaking through the clouds.

The rays of the sun entered my window when the sun rose early in the morning.

From/ Out of nowhere *[Expression] (happening or appearing very suddenly and unexpectedly).*

Tom appeared from/out of nowhere.

He gave me a present out of nowhere.

Impressed *[Adjective] (to have a good feeling on something because it is interesting or beautiful).*

I was impressed with her advanced level of Japanese.

We were very impressed with the accommodation in New York.

I'm really impressed with his house.

Picturesque *[Adjective]* *(attractive or pretty in appearance (of a place, building, scene, etc.)).*

Montenegro has both a mountainous northern region and a picturesque coast.

It was a pretty town with well-preserved buildings and a picturesque harbour.

Ferry *[Noun]* *(a boat or ship that carries people, vehicles or goods across an area of water (a river or a short journey by sea)).*

We took the ferry to a pretty little port city on the island.

I left Hong Kong and took the ferry to Kowloon.

When we took the ferry across the harbor, we saw the Statue of Liberty come into view.

Mainland *[Noun]* *(the main area of land of a country, region, etc).*

This island is joined to the mainland of Friesland.

We took a ferry from the island to the mainland.

I took a plane back to the mainland.

Scenery *[Noun]* *(the beautiful natural features of a place or area, such as mountains, forests, seas, rivers, etc).*

The sheer beauty of the scenery took my breath away.

The scenery here is magnificent.

Overseas *[Adverb]* *(to or in another country, especially one beyond or across the sea; abroad).*

She went overseas to teach ESL after finishing her Linguistics degree.

Generally speaking, Japanese cars are popular overseas.

Some students who study foreign languages decide to go overseas to study.

Breathtaking *[Adjective] (very beautiful, exciting or impressive).*

All suites offer a breathtaking view of the ocean and the mountain.

From this hill, people get a breathtaking view of the city at night.

Crystal clear *[Adjective] (completely or transparently clear and bright).*

The picture on this TV is crystal clear.

The water is crystal clear and slow moving.

Stretch *[Verb] (to extend in length of land or sea).*

The sea stretches along a coastline.

The desert stretches out beyond the horizon.

Endlessly *[Adverb] (seems to have no end or limit).*

The trees along the canal seemed to march endlessly into the distance.

Fields stretched endlessly into the distance.

Peter talked endlessly about his flower garden.

Attract more visitors *[Verb] (to get more people to come to visit).*

The Great Smoky Mountains National Park attracts more visitors each year than any other national park.

Investing in park improvements attracts more visitors.

It can be a huge challenge to remember or memorize the correct meanings of those words.

Show up *[Verb] (to arrive somewhere in order to meet someone).*

It was raining heavily, so only a few people showed up on time.

He showed up late as usual.

It was around midnight when he showed up.

Sandcastle *[Noun] (a small castlelike structure built out of sand, typically by children).*

A summer's day of sailing and building sandcastles.

Our kids like going to the beach and they like making sandcastles.

Check into *[Verb] (to arrive and register at a hotel).*

I checked into a motel and went right to sleep.

We checked into a small hotel and stayed for several days.

Fall away *[Verb] (to disappear).*

Do what you love and the stress falls away.

Full moon *[Noun] (the moon which is shaped like a complete disc and fully illuminated).*

There is a full moon tonight.

We drank tea and saw the full moon last night.

Campfire *[Noun] (an open-air fire that is made when you are camping).*

We were cooking dinner over a campfire.

We were sitting around the campfire and telling scary stories.

To twinkle *[Verb] (to shine and sparkle with a flickering gleam of light).*

The stars twinkled brightly in the sky.

When she smiled, her eyes twinkled with amusement.

To feel at peace *[Verb] (to feel peaceful, without any anxiety or distress).*

She felt at peace when she was meditating.

We felt at peace and welcomed warmly!

Unforgettable *[Adjective] (if something is unforgettable, you can't forget it).*

The trip to our countryside was unforgettable.

My first-time scuba diving was unforgettable.

Jump at the chance *[Verb] (to immediately seize an opportunity).*

He jumped at the chance of a trip to New York.

He jumped at the chance/opportunity to show his boss what he could do.

She jumped at the offer of a better job.

A riot of colour *[Noun] (a collection of many different colours).*

The whole garden was a riot of colour.

The flower-beds were a riot of colour.

Striking *[Adjective] (very attractive and unusual).*

It was a striking outfit which made her feel good.

Flowerbed *[Noun] (a piece of a garden in which flowers are planted).*

His dog came into my garden this morning and buried a bone in my flowerbed.

A leisurely stroll *[Noun] (a slow, relaxing walk).*

After lunch, we went for a leisurely stroll.

My family was enjoying a leisurely stroll in the sunshine.

Avidly *[Adverb] (showing great interest or enthusiasm in).*

She read the book avidly from the beginning to the end.

Tom played game avidly from morning until late in the evening.

Wonderland *[Noun] (an imaginary place in children's stories which is full of wonderful things).*

The city was a wonderland for me to live in.

The fair was a wonderland for both children and adults.

Unique *[Adjective] (very special and unlike anything else).*

His technique was unique and absolutely amazing.

Each person's genetic code is unique.

Pleasant *[Adjective] (nice and enjoyable).*

Yesterday was a pleasant day.

What a pleasant weather it is!

Give someone a lift *[Expression] (give someone a ride).*

I gave her a lift home.

It was David who gave me a lift this morning.

Drop someone off *[Expression] (to take someone to a particular place).*

I dropped her off at college.

I dropped him off at home.

Impression *[Noun] (feeling or feelings about something).*

My first impression of her was that she was a kind and thoughtful young woman.

What was your first impression of Paris?

My impression of Paris is very good.

Get familiar with *[Expression] (familiarize yourself).*

I got familiar with the rhythm and sounds of the language I spoke.

A myriad of *[Adjective]* *(a lot of/ many)*.

The menu at the Chinese restaurant offers a myriad of options.

There is a myriad of species.

Favorable conditions *[Noun]* *(good conditions)*.

The employees have favorable conditions of service.

The location offers favorable conditions for the illegal crossing of goods over the border.

Stimulating *[Adjective]* *(describing something that inspires new ideas or enthusiasm)*.

I had a very stimulating conversation with Mary.

Aerobics is one of the most stimulating forms of exercise.

Golden opportunity *[Noun]* *(a very good opportunity or a chance to do something)*.

He missed golden opportunity to join the Military Academy.

That was a golden opportunity to invest and export into new markets.

Breeze *[Noun]* *(a very soft and gently wind)*.

It's like a cool breeze on a hot summer day.

The flower moved as if caught in a breeze.

Dawn *[Noun]* *(the very early time in the morning when sunlight first begins to appear)*.

The dawn brought cool air and dense fog.

He works from dawn till dusk.

Therapeutic *[Adjective]* *(making someone more relaxed or happier)*.

Meditation can be very therapeutic in helping people to reduce their stress.

Inspire *[Verb]* *(to make someone feel excited or interested in doing something)*.

This video really inspired me to do some really creative activities with my student.

I was really inspired by her teaching way.

Vacation *[Noun]* *(a period of time when a person travels to another place to relax and enjoy himself/ herself)*.

I think we need a vacation.

My vacation went by quickly.

Holiday *[Noun]* *(a period of time you are off from work to go on a trip for relaxation)*.

He seems very tired at the moment. He needs a holiday.

We are going on holiday next week.

Frame of mind *[Noun]* *(the mood that someone is in)*.

I'm not in the right frame of mind to start doing my homework.

He returned from dinner in a happier frame of mind.

Exhilarating *[Adjective]* *(making someone feel extremely happy and excited)*.

The movie was so exhilarating.

He found the experience exhilarating.

Invigorating *[Adjective]* *(making someone feel excited, healthy and full of energy)*.

Exercise is invigorating.

Taking a swim in the sea is very invigorating.

Invaluable *[Adjective]* *(extremely useful)*.

The projector is an invaluable classroom resource because it allows students to see what the teacher is doing.

Without his invaluable help, we would not have met the project deadline.

Breath-taking *[Adjective]* *(extremely beautiful in an impressive way)*.

The beach is famous for its breath-taking views.

What a breath-taking view!

(To) charm *[Verb]* *(to please or attract someone in order to make them like you).*

He was charmed by her beauty and wit.

He was charmed by her vivacity and high spirits.

Hectic *[Adjective]* *(very busy, full of activity).*

I have a hectic schedule for the next few days.

Bangkok is a great city but also a very hectic city.

Valuable *[Adjective]* *(worth a lot of money or important).*

A lot of valuable advice can be found in this book.

We learned a valuable lesson.

Enchanting *[Adjective]* *(very charming or attractive).*

What an enchanting little boy!

The girl looked enchanting in a pale blue dress.

Company *[Noun]* *(the fact of being with a person or people).*

Tom said he wanted some company.

Peter came to stay for a week as company for my mother while I was away.

Appealing *[Adjective]* *(attractive or interesting).*

It doesn't sound too appealing.

He found something about her very appealing and always wanted to be with her.

Renowned *[Adjective]* *(famous for something).*

He is renowned for his patience.

The city is renowned for its terrible air pollution.

Tranquility *[Noun]* *(the state of being quiet and peaceful).*

The city was finally restored to tranquility.

We all like the tranquility of the country life.

Ample *[Adjective]* *(enough or more than enough).*

The light in the room is more than ample.

There were ample food and drinks at the party.

Spacious *[Adjective]* *(large and with plenty of space).*

His house has a spacious kitchen and dining area.

The children occupied the large and spacious classroom.

Glory *[Noun]* *(great beauty).*

The glory of the town is its fountain.

Relic *[Noun]* *(an object surviving from the past that continues to exist).*

We discovered relics of an ancient civilization.

The relics are credited with miraculous powers.

Monotonous *[Adjective]* *(dull, tedious, boring).*

It's monotonous work, like most factory jobs.

He has a very monotonous voice;

Dreary *[Adjective]* *(boring and making you feel sad or unhappy).*

The sky was dreary with heavy rain and gray clouds.

After the death of her mother, she was in a dreary mood for weeks.

Impression *[Noun]* *(feeling or feelings about something or someone).*

His impression of her was favorable.

My impression of the United States is very good.

That day left a deep impression on us.

Hospitality *[Noun] (friendly and generous behavior toward visitors, guests, or clients).*

We received the hospitality of the family.

Thanks for your hospitality over the past few weeks.

 (To) cater for *[Verb] (to provide the things that people need or want).*

The school aims to cater for children of all abilities.

To broaden one's literary horizons *[Verb] (to extend the limit of your knowledge, desires or interests by reading widely).*

He is striving to broaden his literary horizons this year by reading these 20 types of books.

He broadened his literary horizons by extensive reading of poetry from Western cultures.

Relics of the past *[Noun] (old objects that have survived from the past).*

We found relics of the past in the historical sites left behind by former civilizations.

Out of this world *[Expression] (used to emphasize how good, beautiful, etc. something is).*

The fantastic meal was out of this world.

The lobster thermidor was out of this world!

The food was out of this world.

The coffee was out of this world, made by the gods (café farmers) of Colombia.

His confidence was out of this world.

Nostalgia *[Noun]* *(a feeling of sadness mixed with pleasure and affection when you think about things that happened).*

If my sister sees the family pictures and videos, nostalgia may help her regain her memory.

He is filled with nostalgia for his own happy college days.

Some people feel nostalgia for their schooldays.

To be thronged with tourists *[Expression]* *(this refers to the situation in which a place has a crowd or large group of people).*

The island was thronged with tourists.

Kerala is thronged with tourists all year around.

In summer, the centre of New York is thronged with tourists and all the hotels are full.

Backpackers *[Noun]* *(people without much money, who travel on holiday carrying all their belongings in a backpack).*

They are backpackers.

Most of the people here are backpackers.

To get away from it all *[Expression]* *(to leave a big city and go to a peaceful place where you can relax).*

I think we need to get away from it all for a while.

The city is so noisy and crowded that we want to get away from it all for a few days.

The holiday of a lifetime *[Noun]* *(a very special holiday or the best holiday that you will ever have (you will only take once))*

Our trip to Florida was the holiday of a lifetime.

Winners of the competition will receive the holiday of a lifetime.

Ethnic groups *[Noun] (a community or group of people who share a common cultural background or tradition).*

These foods are associated with ethnic groups.

In the United States, there are many ethnic groups who come from different countries and cultures.

Remote corners of the world *[Expression] (places in the world which are hard to access due to distance or difficulties of transport to get there).*

As the Internet started spreading to remote corners of the world, information became more accessible by people from different cultures.

Many of these languages are spoken in remote corners of the world.

Draw inspiration from *[Expression] (be inspired by something (to have new ideas or to be creative)).*

The city's architects have drawn inspiration from traditional Arabian cities.

Many famous artists have drawn inspiration from the countryside.

He has drawn inspiration from a poem he saw on her blog.

Destination resorts *[Noun] (a place where tourists like to visit on vacation).*

This terrific resort & spa is a genuine destination resort.

It is widely argued that global tourism has a negative impact on destination resorts and countries.

Rowdy *[Adjective] (noisy, loud, disorder, rough).*

A rowdy group of boys ran through the streets.

The crowd was very rowdy during the protest against the cuts to university funding.

The bus passengers were rowdy.

Drop off *[Verb] (quickly leave someone or something at a place).*

After my wife drops off the kids at school, she usually stops at Starbucks for a cappuccino.

I will pass your house this morning and drop off the wallet that you left at my house.

Pick up *[Verb] (to get or bring someone from somewhere).*

Parents nowadays tend to drop off and pick up their children at the school gate although the school is close to their home.

I pick up my son from school at noon every day.

No-stopping zones = No parking areas *[Noun] (areas in which you are not permitted to stop or park your car or other vehicles).*

No Stopping' zones provided for children's crossings.

Yellow or red lines indicate no-stopping zones.

Slum *[Noun] (an area of a city where living conditions are very poor and the houses are in bad condition).*

I can't stand this slum any longer, tidy it up!

The redevelopment of the slum area is well under way.

Pay a visit *[Expression] (to go somewhere to visit (someone or a place)).*

If you have time, pay a visit to the City Art Gallery.

Are you going to pay a visit to China this fall?

Historical places *[Noun] (places that have historical value due to some important events in the past).*

Both Kuala Lumpur and London are often full of historical places to visit, such as the Tower of London and the Batu Caves.

I want to have a longer vacation in Greece to enjoy more of the historical places.

Local inhabitants *[Noun] (people who live in the town).*

They worked hard, but tended to stay aloof from the local inhabitants.

The local inhabitants do not enjoy having so many tourists in their town.

A thing of the past *[Noun] (something that no longer happens or exists).*

Some traditional family roles and structures have now become a thing of the past.

The times when the teacher had only a blackboard are now a thing of the past in most classrooms.

Glamour *[Noun] (beauty or charm that is sexually attractive and makes something or somebody seem special).*

Youngsters associate Western clothing with glamour, beauty, and success.

She dreams of being a full-time glamour model.

Overcharge *[Verb] (make somebody pay too much for something).*

They tried to overcharge me, but I didn't agree.

Make sure they don't overcharge you for the food and drinks.

Influx *[Noun] (an arrival or entry into a place of large numbers of people or things).*

The influx of tourists has reached its summer peak.

The hotel has received a large influx of guests.

Far-flung *[Adjective] (very distant or remote).*

Email enables far-flung friends to keep in touch.

His fame has reached the most far-flung corners of the globe.

Budget airline *[Noun] (low-cost airline (an airline which offers cheaper tickets)).*

We took a budget airline because we didn't have much luggage.

Travelling with a budget airline is not always comfortable, but it is usually affordable.

Exotic *[Adjective] (something that is exciting and unusual because it is connected with a distant country).*

When she saw the exotic fruit, she was excited about eating something from a different nation.

He dreamed of flying away to exotic faraway places.

Immensely *[Adverb] (vast; huge; to a very great extent).*

She looked immensely relieved when she heard the news.

He was immensely strong.

The cave was immensely deep.

Cuisine *[Noun] (a style of cooking).*

The restaurant is famous for its excellent Korean cuisine.

Our cuisine includes a few hot dishes but it is not always hot.

Costly *[Adjective] (costing a lot of money).*

The furniture in the store was too costly, so she decided not to buy anything.

It is costly and politically difficult to continue this conflict.

Luxury *[Adjective] (something usually very expensive, beautiful or comfortable that you enjoy but do not really need).*

He lives in luxury.

He owns three houses and four luxury cars.

Taking a taxi is a luxury for her.

Tourist attraction *[Noun]* *(a place to visit for pleasure and interest that is very popular with tourists).*

The Statue of Liberty is a major tourist attraction.

The Eiffel Tower in Paris, France, is a popular tourist attraction.

Historic site *[Noun]* *(an official location where pieces of political, military have been preserved).*

We visited the historic sites of the country.

We are going to visit the most important monuments and historic sites in Paris.

Gigantic *[Adjective]* *(extremely large).*

The apple was gigantic.

I love my gigantic, tan dog.

Immense *[Adjective]* *(vast; huge; extremely large in size, amount, or degree).*

He experienced immense relief after it was over.

This device has saved me an immense amount of time.

She seems to take immense pleasure in playing with children.

Essential *[Adjective]* *(completely necessary; extremely important).*

Food is very essential for our body.

Trees are very essential in our lives.

Incredible *[Adjective]* *(surprising, or impossible to believe).*

The chef created an incredible meal that was the best meal I had ever eaten.

The story is incredible.

Refreshing *[Adjective]* *(making someone feel more lively when they have been feeling hot or tired).*

A glass of cold water is very refreshing in hot weather.

A chilled glass of lemonade can be very refreshing on a hot day.

Barbecue *[Noun]* *(a meal or party at which meat and other food are cooked and eaten outside).*

Tom invited us over for some beer and barbecue.

I haven't had a barbecue for a long time.

Buffet *[Noun]* *(a meal at which people serve themselves by going and choosing different types of food).*

Everyone on the cruise ship enjoys the free buffet lunch.

The food was very good, and we had a buffet in the morning and in the evening.

We went into a restaurant and had a buffet.

Picnic *[Noun]* *(a meal eaten outside, especially in the countryside as part of an excursion).*

We decided to have a picnic down by the lake.

One spring day, the school arranged a picnic.

Snack *[Noun]* *(a small portion of food eaten between meals).*

I had a snack before I went back to work.

He didn't have time for lunch so he just grabbed a quick snack.

Ready meal *[Noun]* *(a meal that you buy at a shop already cooked and which you only have to heat it before eating it).*

We just had a ready meal last night.

She would rather have a ready meal of spaghetti bolognese.

All-inclusive *[Adjective]* *(including all the costs, charges, and services of accommodation, meals and drinks).*

In recent years, the all-inclusive vacation package has exploded throughout the Caribbean.

You can now enjoy carefree worldwide all-inclusive holidays whilst maintaining the highest levels of quality.

Half-board *[Adjective]* *(a hotel rate that includes accommodation, breakfast and dinner, but not lunch).*

In their traditional but elegant designed dining room, they offer us their wonderful half-board service.

The farmhouse offers a half board service to families and small groups in some comfortable lodgings and grants a natural and relaxing holiday.

Full-board *[Adjective]* *(the services that you get at a hotel including all your meals there).*

Cost for a course including full board and lodging is $200.

A week at the resort with full-board is certainly more expensive than a week with half-board.

Self-catering *[Adjective]* *(a holiday deal where you can cook your own food (meals are not provided)).*

Tom thinks that self-catering is neither pleasant nor efficient.

To book (something) *[Verb]* *(to reserve (accommodations, a place, etc.) for an event in the future).*

When I book a table at a restaurant, I book it under my surname "Hughes".

Can I book two seats on that flight?

He booked a round-trip flight to Europe.

Charter flight *[Noun]* *(a cheap regular flight).*

There is a wide variety of entertainment options on a charter flight.

Due to their modest budget, they had to take a charter flight.

Far-off destination *[Noun]* *(an exciting place that is far away from where you are).*

Italy is a far-off destination; however, I am going to visit it next month.

Traveling to a far-off destination attracts attention of many young people. It is a really common activity these days.

Getting away from it all *[Expression]* *(to go somewhere different from where you live in order to rest from a daily routine).*

The city is so noisy and crowded that I want to get away from it all.

We've decided to go hiking in the mountains to get away from it all.

Go off the beaten track *[Expression]* *(to visit an isolated place where few people go).*

Unlike his brother, he prefers to go off the beaten track.

It's high time you went off the beaten track!

Guided tour *[Noun]* *(a tour in which a group of people is guided by an expert who explains facts about the place).*

We went on a guided tour of the city.

The guided tour of the site was one of my trip highlights.

The wonders of the temple were made more lucid by a guided tour of the little museum.

Head for *[Verb]* *(go towards a direction).*

I couldn't figure out where on earth he was heading for.

The plane is heading for Dubai at the moment.

Holiday brochure *[Noun]* *(a small book or magazine containing details of the holiday).*

The information provided in your holiday brochure must not be false or misleading.

Our guide gave us a great brochure about our hotel.

Holiday destination *[Noun] (the place to which people are going for a holiday).*

New York is still our most popular holiday destination.

Spain is probably the greatest holiday destination on the planet.

Hordes of tourists *[Noun] (large crowds of tourists).*

There are always hordes of tourists here in the summer.

Hordes of tourists arrive in Italy every June.

In the middle of nowhere *[Adverb] (in a place where few people live that is far away from any towns and cities).*

He lives in a tiny cottage in the middle of nowhere.

They live on a small farm in the middle of nowhere.

Out of season *[Expression] (at a time of the year when a place is less popular).*

Hotels are cheaper out of season.

We spend our holiday out of season.

Package tour *[Noun] (a holiday at a fixed price organized by a travel agent including transportation, accommodations, etc).*

We have a package tour to Bali, which includes airfare, hotel, and guided tours.

A package tour to England can really save you a ton of money.

Picturesque village *[Noun] (a nice, beautiful, attractive village, especially because it is old and interesting).*

The houses were in a picturesque village.

My parents live in a picturesque village.

Places of interest *[Noun] (a place that is famous for its scenery or historical sites).*

Your tour to Singapore will never be complete unless you visit our places of interest.

My native city has a variety of places of interest.

Tourist trap *[Noun] (a place such as a restaurant, shop, or hotel that is visited by many tourists and usually is expensive).*

Endangered animals caught in the tourist trap.

We've visited many tourist traps recently.

Wildlife safari *[Noun] (an observational holiday, mainly in Africa).*

The village is surrounded by wildlife/safari areas, and very few people live there.

We'd love to go on a wildlife safari sometime.

Youth hostel *[Noun] (a cheap hotel where young people can stay for a short period of time).*

Is there a youth hostel around here?

The youth hostel used to be an office building.

Remote *[Adjective] (far away from places where most people live).*

They live in a remote community in the desert.

My grandparents were from a remote village in Vietnam.

Coastal *[Adjective] (on land beside a sea (the land near a shore)).*

Our coastal area provides a variety of opportunities for recreation.

San Diego is a coastal city in the state of California.

Mountainous *[Adjective] (covered with mountains; having a lot of mountains).*

The town is in a mountainous district.

The countryside is more mountainous in the north.

Much of the earth's surface is mountainous.

Rural *[Adjective]* *(relating to the countryside, far away from large towns or cities).*

The area is still very rural and undeveloped.

My family used to live in a very rural area of the Czech Rep.

Urban *[Adjective]* *(relating to towns and cities).*

Most Chinese cities are very dense and very urban.

I've always wanted to live in an urban area.

Means of transport *[Noun]* *(all different types of transport that you can travel or carry goods in).*

I use a car as a means of transport.

What means of transport will you use to get to the airport?

Tourist *[Noun]* *(someone who is visiting a place for pleasure on holiday).*

In the summer, the museum is filled with tourists.

Our city attracts a lot of tourists every day.

Go skiing/ skating/ fishing/ trekking (go + … ing)

I used to go skiing in the winter.

We used to go skating every weekend.

When I was a child, I used to go fishing with my dad.

We want to go trekking in the mountains.

MUSIC

Concert venue *[Noun]* *(a location used for a concert or musical performance).*

I had an opportunity to attend that concert venue.

They are going to play in that new concert venue in town.

Classical music *[Noun]* *(music that is developed from a European tradition mainly in the 18th and 19th centuries.)*

My girlfriend likes pop music but I prefer classical music.

Classical music is my father's cup of tea.

Pop music *[Noun]* *(a type of music that is popular with many people at a particular time).*

The best part about pop music is that you can find lyrics for songs almost anywhere on the Internet.

Pop music is deriving from rock and roll.

Folk music *[Noun]* *(traditional music in a particular country, region, or community).*

He plays folk music with guitar accompaniment.

I used to like folk music.

Hip-hop *[Noun]* *(a style of music usually based on rap in which the words are spoken rather than sung).*

Hip-hop is my brother favorite type of music.

Soothing *[Adjective]* *(making someone feel calm and more relaxed).*

I often listen to soothing music in order to relax.

In order to relax, he usually listens to soothing music.

Melody = rhyme *[Noun] (a tune).*

It is a simple melody with complex harmonies.

I love that song. It has a pleasant melody.

Contemporary music *[Noun] (modern music).*

The older generation prefers to listen to music from the 1970's and the 1980's while young people tend to prefer contemporary music.

Genres of music *[Noun] (particular types or styles of music).*

The album covers a range of different genres of music.

Nowadays there are more genres of music out there than what we really know about.

Catchy melody *[Noun] (a melody that is pleasing and easily remembered).*

Due to its simple and catchy melody, this song became very popular.

My kids really love the fast-moving catchy melody. It looks like

Meaningful lyrics *[Noun] (words in a song that are meaningful).*

Not all pop music has interesting or meaningful lyrics.

This song has meaningful lyrics but difficult to understand.

Musical instrument *[Noun] (an object such as a violin, piano, flute or drum that you use to make music).*

My favorite musical instrument is the trumpet.

This musical instrument is a stringed instrument.

Enrich *[Verb] (to make something better or to improve the quality of something).*

Music can certainly enrich our whole life.

We can enrich our mind by reading.

Hi-fi devices *[Noun]* *(equipment which plays recorded music).*

Waves from hi-fi devices also tend to cause headaches if used for too long.

It is one of the smallest portable hi-fi devices.

Enlighten *[Verb]* *(to give someone information, knowledge and understanding about something).*

The teacher's job was to enlighten her students on the various theories of physical science.

Can you enlighten who is at fault?

The teacher tried to enlighten everyone with his teachings.

Rock music *[Noun]* *(music that is developed from rock 'n' roll).*

I really love rock music, especially alternative and hard rock.

People who love rock music shouldn't have outdoor parties.

Catchy tune *[Noun]* *(a song that is pleasing and easily remembered.)*

It was a song with a catchy tune.

I love the catchy tune in that short video.

Live music *[Noun]* *(music played on instruments in front of an audience.)*

It's hard to find a club which performs live music in this area.

Peter likes to go to a local jazz club where he can enjoy live music.

Music to one's ears *[Expression]* *(something that is very pleasant and enjoyable to hear).*

Her news is music to my ears.

Their offer of help was music to my ears.

His words were music to my ears.

Have a rehearsal *[Expression] (a practice or trial performance of something (a play, dance, etc.) in preparation for a public performance).*

We had a rehearsal dinner for our son's wedding and it was perfect!

We never had a rehearsal, but fortunately, it all worked out.

Opera *[Noun] (a kind of performance performed by singers and an orchestra).*

I want to go to the opera so I can have a good evening out.

She likes to go to the opera; in fact, it's her favorite type of entertainment.

Ringtone *[Noun] (a sound made by a mobile phone when someone is calling).*

How can I change the ringtone to vibration?

He sets his favourite song as a ringtone on his cell phone.

Melodious *[Adjective] (music which has a pleasant tune (very pleasant to listen to)).*

He has a melodious singing voice.

She is a melodious singer.

This piece of music is melodious.

Live concert *[Noun] (a music performance given by one or more singers that is taking place).*

There are over 15 million video streams during the live concert.

Rock band *[Noun] (a band of musicians who play rock music together).*

That rock band gives her a headache.

He plays in a rock band.

Tuneful *[Adjective] (producing a pleasant sound/tune; melodious).*

Being wonderfully melodic and tuneful, his songs have made me weep.

The music for the film is quite tuneful.

To face the music *[Verb] (be confronted with the unpleasant consequences of something you have done wrong).*

After drinking alcohol all night, the next morning he had to face the music.

He's been caught cheating. He must face the music.

To ring a bell *[Verb] (to sound familiar).*

I think I heard this song somewhere. It definitely rings a bell.

The man's name rings a bell but I can't remember him.

To sound like a broken record *[Expression] (someone who keeps annoying you by saying the same thing over and over again).*

He sounds like a broken record and that annoys most people.

My little brother sounds like a broken record.

To strike (hit) a false note *[Expression] (to do something wrong; to behave inappropriately).*

Occasionally, he hits a false note.

When I hit a false note, he knows.

FOOD

Pour *[Verb]* *(to make a liquid flow into a container).*

Pour some milk into a coffee mug, please.

Pour some tea into the cups.

Leftover food *[Noun]* *(the food that remains after a meal).*

Tom fed his leftover food to his dog.

They always have leftover food.

Catering food *[Verb]* *(serving food).*

A tray for catering food or drinks.

Cuisine *[Noun]* *(a style or method of cooking in a certain place).*

This restaurant is famous for its spicy cuisine.

The city is known for its excellent and diverse cuisine

Veggie *[Noun]* *(vegetable).*

He likes cheese, veggie, and I like fish.

We grow our own veggies at home.

Vegan *[Noun]* *(a person who does not consume animal products (such as meat, eggs, or dairy products)).*

He decided to turn vegan after watching a video about how poultry is raised.

He was a poet, an anarchist, and a vegan.

Succulent *[Adjective]* *(juicy and tasty).*

The restaurant is famous for its succulent chocolate cake.

The apple was very succulent.

Delectable *[Adjective]* (delicious).

He could not stop eating the delectable dish.

Warm cookies make a delectable snack.

Healthy eating habits *[Noun]* *(eating healthy food at regular times of the day).*

We have good food and stay healthy eating habits.

Many people realize that healthy eating habits can help support a healthy weight.

A vegetarian diet *[Noun]* *(a diet focuses on plants for food without any meat, poultry, or seafood).*

Since a vegetarian diet is believed to be better for heath, many people, nowadays, tend to choose to become vegetarians.

A vegetarian diet has been found to reduce the risk of heart disease, obesity, and some types of cancer.

Plant foods *[Noun]* *(a number of types of food derived from plants, including vegetables, whole grains, nuts, seeds, etc).*

Seaweed is one of the rare plant foods that contains DHA with many health benefits.

Protein is found in a wide variety of both animal and plant foods.

Organic plant foods are manufactured without using conventional fertilizers and pesticides.

To be high in fiber *[Expression]* *(nondigestible part of food that helps to keep a person healthy by moving other food quickly through the body).*

My mom tends to choose foods that are high in fiber and low in calories.

All grains are high in fiber, but not all of them are packed with nutrition.

Inadequate *[Adjective]* *(not enough in quantity or not good enough in quality).*

His clothing was inadequate for the harsh weather conditions.

The water supply is inadequate to provide water for all the people in the city.

Our school facilities are inadequate for foreign students.

Tasty *[Adjective] (having a very pleasant and delicious flavor).*

The restaurant serves a lot of tasty food for customers.

These apples are tasty to eat.

Fattening *[Adjective] (likely to make you fat easily).*

Unfortunately, potato chips are fattening.

These cakes are very fattening - do not eat too many!

Food hygiene *[Noun] (the clean and safety of food from production to consumption).*

Consumers shall have the right to be informed of food hygiene and safety, to select and use proper food;

If you want to teach your children about food hygiene, start with the basics – talk to them about bacteria and germs.

Appetizing *[Adjective] (smelling or looking attractive, appealing to or stimulating your taste, so that you feel hungry or thirsty).*

The meal the children made didn't look very appetizing, but it tasted pretty good.

The roast beef is very appetizing.

Ripe *[Adjective] ((of fruit or crops) to be fully grown and ready to eat).*

The rice is ripe for harvest.

My kids actually like the taste of ripe cherries.

Make sure the plums are fully ripe before you eat them.

Overcooked *[Adjective]* *(to spoil food by cooking it for longer than necessary)*.

The chicken is overcooked.

Some of the meat is overcooked.

Grill *[Verb]* *(to broil or cook something on a grill)*.

I am grilling fish.

A chef needs to learn chopping, roasting, and grilling.

Roast *[Verb]* *(to cook meat in an oven or over an open fire)*.

He nearly dropped the plate of roast beef.

I personally would rather roast a chicken whole.

My aunt and uncle made a delicious roast beef for dinner when we visited them.

Steam *[Verb]* *(the hot wet substance like a thin cloud that is produced when water boils)*.

My girlfriend prefers to steam carrots rather than boil them.

Steamed fish and vegetables.

Stew *[Verb]* *(to cook (meat, fruit, or other food) slowly in liquid)*.

Stew *[Noun]* *(a dish of (meat, fruit, or other food) cooked slowly in liquid)*.

I'm making a stew for lunch.

She served him a bowl of beef stew.

Portion *[Noun]* *(a part of a whole; an amount, or total)*.

She only eats a small portion of food.

Have you eaten your portion of vegetables today?

Spoonful *[Noun]* *(the amount of a substance that a spoon can hold)*.

Tom ate a spoonful of peanut butter.

A spoonful of honey.

A spoonful of sugar.

Bitter *[Adjective]* *(something has a strong sharp taste or smell that is not sweet).*

The flavours are sweet, sour, salty, and bitter.

Many customers in the restaurant found the coffee too bitter to drink.

Crunchy *[Adjective]* *(making a loud noise when bitten or crushed).*

The fruit's flesh is crunchy and watery in texture, similar to cucumber.

I love the crunchy texture of fresh lettuce.

Tom ate crispy, crunchy cookies.

Salty *[Adjective]* *(containing salt, or tasting like salt).*

They gave him salty water to make him vomit.

Sea water is salty.

Savory *[Adjective]* *((of food) be salty or spicy rather than sweet).*

Do you prefer sweet or savory food?

The steak is very savory; the flavor is tremendous.

Spicy *[Adjective]* *(spicy food means the food has a strong hot flavor).*

The ginger gives the dish a wonderful spicy flavour.

She's used to eating spicy food every day.

Homemade food *[Noun]* *(food that is prepared at home, in a traditional way, by a real person).*

There's nothing like mom's homemade food to cheer you up.

What kinds of homemade food do you like?

Nutritious *[Adjective]* *(providing the substances that you need in order to be healthy).*

Wholemeal bread is more nutritious than white bread.

Doing lots of exercises won't keep you healthy if you don't eat nutritious food as well.

Nutritious foods help us to maintain good health.

Dine in *[Verb]* *(to have dinner at home, instead of at a restaurant).*

We're dining in tonight.

The coupon can only be used when dining in at ABC.

Dine out *[Verb]* *(to have dinner at a restaurant, instead of at home).*

Instead of dining out, we ordered a couple of pizzas.

Dining out frequently is expensive.

We eat at home a lot, so dining out sometimes is a nice change.

Fussy eater *[Noun]* *(someone who is very picky about the food, eats very few things and constantly complains about the food).*

Her husband is a very fussy eater, and he's never pleased with her cooking.

He eats anything. He's not a fussy eater.

Home-cooked food *[Noun]* *((of food) prepared or cooked at home).*

I love home-cooked food. My favourite dish is Clarissa's fried rice.

I love to try new recipes, and I love home-cooked food that tastes really good.

In a walking distance of *[Expression]* *(near; close to).*

We usually dine at a restaurant that's in a walking distance of our home.

Mouth-watering *[Adjective]* *((of food) smelling, looking, or sounding delicious, appetizing).*

The waitress came round with a tray of mouth-watering cream cakes.

There is plenty of mouth-watering, delicious food on the table.

Processed food [Noun] (food that has been treated or prepared in an unhealthy way to achieve its current state).

Pure food is safer and more filling than processed food.

We eat more processed food than natural food.

Quick snack [Noun] (a small portion of food that is eaten quickly between meals).

There's enough time for a quick snack.

We didn't have time for lunch so we just grabbed a quick snack.

Restrain one's hunger [Verb] (if you restrain your hunger, you try to avoid eating when you are hungry).

Tom could not restrain his hunger and immediately went to the nearest fast-food restaurant.

The girl was unable to restrain her hunger.

Slap-up meal [Noun] (a large and very good meal).

I had a slap up meal and a nice few bottles of beer while I was watching sport on TV.

He greeted us like old friends and we had a slap up meal like the old time.

Starving hungry [Adjective] (to be extremely hungry).

I was starving hungry and ate the whole roast chicken.

I'm starving hungry. Where can I get something to eat?

The main meal [Noun] (the most important or largest meal of the day).

We usually have our main meal of the day in the evening.

She made chicken for the main meal.

To be dying of hunger *[Expression]* *(feeling very hungry)*.

They are scared of dying of hunger.

He hasn't eaten all day. He is dying of hunger!

To eat a balanced diet *[Expression]* *(to eat correctly with proper quantities)*.

It is important to eat a balanced diet and control portion size.

I try to drink plenty of water and eat a balanced diet with lots of leafy greens.

To eat like a horse *[Expression]* *(to eat a lot)*.

She's very thin but she eats like a horse!

If you are very hungry, you can eat like a horse.

To follow a recipe *[Expression]* *(to cook a meal following a set of instructions)*.

When she bakes a cake, she follows a recipe.

Carmen always follows a recipe when she makes a cake.

To foot the bill *[Expression]* *(to pay the bill; to pay for something)*.

You paid for lunch last week. Let me foot the bill for dinner tonight.

She ordered drinks and then left him to foot the bill!

To grab a bite to eat *[Expression]* *(to eat something in a hurry)*.

I need a few minutes to grab a bite to eat.

I usually grab a bite to eat before I see a movie.

Let's grab a bite to eat if you didn't have lunch yet.

To have a sweet tooth *[Expression]* *(to enjoy eating sweet food)*.

I have a sweet tooth, so I will definitely have dessert!

Mary eats candy all the time. She must have a sweet tooth.

To play with your food *[Expression] (to push food around the plate without eating it).*

He plays with his food, and all he wants is his milk.

She just plays with her food, she's not really hungry.

To spoil your appetite *[Expression] (to make you want to eat less).*

I didn't take biscuits, as it will spoil my appetite when I go for lunch.

The school-age kid spoils his appetite for dinner because he ate too many snacks after school.

To wine and dine *[Expression] (to entertain someone with food and drink, usually at a fancy restaurant).*

He has not had a chance to wine and dine with her yet.

The company wined and dined the prospective clients.

Ingredients *[Noun] (substances that you use in making a particular meal).*

The ingredients for this recipe are a little expensive.

She tried to turn her ingredients into delicious meals.

Speciality *[Noun] (a type of food that a particularly place is famous for, because it is extremely good).*

Pancakes are my speciality.

Oysters are a local speciality of the area.

Overeating *[Noun] (the act of consuming more food than your body needs).*

Habitual overeating had distended the boy's stomach.

She is sick from overeating.

Obese people find it difficult to stop overeating.

TECHNOLOGY

Computer age *[Noun] (the period in modern history characterized by the development and widespread use of computers).*

Living in a computer age has both many benefits and problems.

The rate of cybercrime is significantly increasing in the computer age.

Computer buff *[Noun] (a user who is very enthusiastic about computers).*

Tom is a computer buff, so when my laptop has problems I ask him for help.

Desktop PC *[Noun] (a personal computer that remains on a desk and it is designed to be used by one person at home or in an office).*

My laptop is not detecting AVRduino but my desktop PC does.

This laptop computer is better than my desktop PC.

He loves his desktop PC and uses it more than his Laptop.

Gadget *[Noun] (a small device or machine that has a particular purpose, like a smartphone).*

The most important gadget for me is a laptop.

This laptop is the most expensive gadget I have bought.

Geek *[Noun] (someone who is really interested in technology, especially computers).*

My neighbor is a real geek so fixing the Internet connection was a breeze.

Jeannie is a real geek; she loves gaming.

Technology gadget *[Noun] (a small device or machine that has a particular function).*

My brother is interested in technology gadgets.

Subscriber *[Noun] (someone who pays to regularly receive or access a service).*

The number of subscribers who opted out increased last month.

All subscribers receive a FREE monthly e-book.

To utilize *[Verb] (to use).*

We had better utilize our natural resources.

Smiley *[Noun] (a symbol representing a smiling face that is used online by users).*

I sent a smiley face in response to her message.

The boy captioned the picture with a smiley face.

Online *[Noun] (on the Internet).*

She loves chatting online in her free time.

All documentation can be found online for free.

Advances in technology *[Noun] (improvements, innovations or developments in technology).*

There have been so many advances in technology over the last ten years, it's almost hard to keep up with all the changes.

Advances in technology can make running your company easier and less expensive.

Digital age *[Noun] (a period when information is sent electronically).*

We live in a digital age, where technology is intrinsic to our daily lives.

Do schools still need paper textbooks in a digital age?

Reliance [on] *[Noun] (a synonym for "dependence on": the state of needing something or someone all the time in order to survive or be successful).*

There is more reliance on computers in education nowadays.

Our reliance on smartphones and other devices will likely only continue to rise.

Innovation *[Noun] (a new method, idea, equipment etc).*

The rapid pace of technological innovation.

They are responsible for many innovations in their field.

Digital camera *[Noun] (a camera that records and stores digital pictures and video in the form of electronic signals that can be looked at on a computer).*

He is using a digital camera to take pictures.

This digital camera has a setting for white balance that you can adjust for the warmness of the light.

To back up files *[Verb] (to make a copy of files on your computer in case of its problem).*

He had to back up files on his computer because he was going to reinstall his operating system.

Weekly, I back up files on my computer to an external hard disk.

To be stuck behind a computer *[Expression] (to use computer for a long period of time).*

I don't want my son stuck behind a computer; he should be outside playing.

A lot of students are stuck behind their computers all day.

To boot up *[Verb] (to start a computer).*

I booted up my computer and checked my email.

He woke up this morning and booted up his computer to begin working on his college homework.

To go online *[Verb] (to use the Internet).*

I usually go online in the evening.

Millions of people go online every day.

FRIENDS

Close friends *[Noun]* *(friends who know and understand each other very well).*

He and I have been close friends for over 20 years.

She has two really close friends; one is a doctor and the other is a lawyer.

Mutual friend *[Noun]* *(a friend who is shared by two people).*

Peter and I became acquainted through our mutual friends.

We met through a mutual friend.

Get on with *[Expression]* *(to have a friendly relationship with them).*

Tom gets on well with his boss.

I get on well with my parents.

To create a strong bond *[Verb]* *(to make a strong connection with someone or animal).*

I have created a strong bond with my dog.

I usually make a phone call to my parents because I have a strong bond with them.

Compliment *[Noun]* *(an expression of praise or admiration for someone).*

He complimented me on my dress.

Jessica blushed when I complimented her hair.

Sound advice *[Noun]* *(good advice).*

My uncle gave me sound advice about my choice of career.

The doctor gave the patient sound advice about healthy eating.

Care about *[Verb] (to be concerned about someone or something).*

Her parents are only doing this because they care about her.

No one seemed to care about his feelings.

The doctor advised her to take exercise and care about her health.

Console *[Verb] (to give sympathy to comfort someone who is sad or disappointed).*

We consoled her with a sympathy card and flowers.

They consoled him by telling him to have patience.

Circle of virtual friends *[Noun] (a group of friends whom you chat with online).*

Her circle of virtual friends was immense.

Facebook is a social network which has a wide circle of virtual friends that youngsters can access and discover many friends.

Enjoy each other's company *[Expression] (to enjoy spending time with each other).*

Tom and Mary enjoy each other's company.

It is true that they enjoy each other's company.

We will enjoy each other's company for the rest of our lives.

Fair-weather friend *[Noun] (someone who only wants to be your good friend when you are cheerful and successful).*

He has realized that Bill is a fair-weather friend.

I am looking for a loyal friend, not a fair-weather friend.

Best friend *[Noun] (a closest and dearest friend).*

His name is Tony. He is my best friend.

I consider him as my best friend.

Even though Tom used to be my best friend, I'm beginning to hate him.

Soul mate *[Noun] (someone with whom you have a special relationship with because you share the same feelings, attitudes, and beliefs).*

Tom has been my soul mate for a long time.

She is my wife, my best friend, and my soul mate.

Get in touch with somebody *[Expression] (to contact somebody by talking or writing).*

He plans to get in touch with his friends when he returns home.

I'll get in touch with Tom by telephone tomorrow.

Near and dear to someone *[Expression] (to have a very close relationship with someone).*

Our brand is very near and dear to us.

His baseball card collection was near and dear to him.

Coffee is very near and dear to me.

Shoulder to cry on *[Expression] (someone who is always ready to listen to your problems and give you sympathy, emotional support, etc).*

I just wanted a shoulder to cry on.

Lucy's father died yesterday. She needs a shoulder to cry on.

To be through thick and thin *[Expression] (if you stay with someone through thick and thin, you always support or stay with them under all circumstances, no matter how difficult).*

In marriage, you have to stick together through thick and thin.

He stood beside his friend through thick and thin.

To be well-matched *[Adjective] ((of two people) to be similar in interests).*

Tom and Mary are well-matched as a couple.

I would probably say that my sister and her husband are well matched.

To fall for someone (to fall in love with someone) *[Expression] (to start to love someone).*

The moment he met his wife, I fell for her completely.

She fell for him the moment she saw him.

To get on like a house on fire *[Expression] ((of two people) to like each other very much and have a very good and friendly relationship very quickly).*

Bill and Jack have a lot of same interests and get on like a house on fire.

He bought me a drink and we got on like a house on fire.

To get to know someone *[Expression] (to become acquainted; start to be familiar with someone).*

I did not have the opportunity to get to know him.

I got to know her in primary school.

To have a lot in common *[Expression] ((of two people) share similar interests, beliefs, attitudes, opinions, etc).*

Tom and Mary have a lot in common.

My brother and I used to have a lot in common when we were younger.

To hit it off with somebody *[Expression]* (to quickly like someone when you meet him/her for the first time).

I didn't really hit it off with her friends.

These children hit it off well in the kindergarten.

To lose touch with someone *[Expression] (to stop communicating with someone, usually because you lose their contact).*

I lost touch with Peter after he moved to Canada.

He lost touch with his college roommate after graduation.

TOWNS AND CITIES

Cosmopolitan *[Noun] (including people from many different countries and cultures).*

Singapore is considered as one of the most cosmopolitan cities in the world.

London is a truly cosmopolitan city.

Situated *[Verb] (in a particular place or position).*

The school is situated near the park.

Paris is situated in northern France.

Population *[Noun] (all the people living in a particular town, area, or country).*

The population of the nearest big city was growing.

In spite of the significant growth in population, the healthcare facilities are extremely insufficient.

Specialty *[Noun] (a product that is extremely good in a particular place).*

Wood carving is a specialty of this village.

Oysters are a local specialty of the area.

Cost of living *[Noun] (the level of prices you pay for basic things such as food, clothes, shelter, and transport).*

It is the fact that the cost of living is always rising.

The cost of living has increased dramatically.

City dwellers *[Noun] (people who live in a city).*

He is a city dweller, so he has no idea on how to milk a cow.

City dwellers are suggested to produce fewer greenhouse-gas emissions than those who live in the countryside.

Air quality *[Noun] (the state of the air around us (how much pollution it contains)).*

A large amount of harmful pollutants have a detrimental effect on air quality.

Open the windows to circulate the air on days when the air quality is good.

Nightlife *[Noun] (evening entertainment in places such as theaters, nightclubs, and bars).*

Havana, which is the capital of Cuba, has a lively nightlife.

I've always found it a friendly place and has a good nightlife.

Vibrant *[Adjective] (lively and exciting (full of energy and enthusiasm)).*

The vibrant streets of a big city.

Orange is a very vibrant and energetic color.

Dynamic *[Adjective] (very lively and enthusiastic).*

He is very dynamic and motivated to get the job.

We are in a dynamic group of people.

Holiday resort (tourist resort) *[Noun] (a place where lots of people go for a holiday).*

Ischia is a popular seaside holiday resort.

Rimini is a thriving holiday resort on the east coast of Italy.

Seaside resort *[Noun] (a resort town or resort hotel, located on the coast where people spend holidays).*

A sandy beach at a seaside resort area.

Fill your break with fun and activity at a seaside resort.

Be crazy about *[Verb] (to be very interested or very enthusiastic about something).*

He is crazy about skiing.

She's completely crazy about him.

Spare time *[Noun]* *(leisure time (time when you do not have to work or study)).*

My mom loves to read books on cooking in her spare time.

In my spare time, I'm quite into listening to music.

Check-in desk *[Noun]* *(the place at the airport where you register for your flight and deposit your luggage).*

I'll meet you at the check-in desk.

The check-in desk is located in the lobby.

Sunbathe *[Verb]* *(to sit or lie in the sun, especially to make your skin darker).*

Tom was sunbathing on the dock.

They're sunbathing around the pool.

Get a suntan *[Verb]* *(to make your skin darker).*

She doesn't want to get a suntan.

Tom is such a beach bum. All he wants to do is getting a suntan.

Destination *[Noun]* *(the place to which someone or something is going or travelling).*

Although each person follows a different path, our destinations are the same.

The most beautiful destination I've been to was the Seychelles Islands.

Travel agency *[Noun]* *(an agency that helps travelers plan holidays and make travel arrangements, especially transportation, accommodations, tours, and trips).*

Almost 70% of tourists do not use a travel agency.

Expedia is the largest online travel agency in the world.

Tour guide *[Noun]* *(a person employed to show tourists around places of interest and explain its history, architecture etc).*

She was previously employed as a tour guide.

Our tour guide showed us around the old town.

Package holiday *[Noun]* *(a vacation arranged by a travel company for a fixed price, with arrangements for transportation, accommodations, and sometimes meals and entertainment).*

We went on a cheap package holiday to Majorca.

We're going on a package holiday to Hong Kong.

Hitchhike *[Verb]* *(to travel by asking someone to take you in their vehicle).*

The man hitchhiked to get home after his car broke down.

Sometimes he hitchhiked to a car, and sometimes he hitchhiked to a truck.

Set off *[Verb]* *(to start a journey; to start to go somewhere).*

After making sure she was sound asleep, he crept out of the room and set off.

I'm just about to set off for the station.

Campsite *[Noun]* *(a place where people on holiday use for camping).*

The campsite is in a beautiful location next to the beach.

The campsite is close to all local amenities.

Adjacent *[Adverb]* *(next to or close to something else).*

He couldn't sleep because of the noise coming from the adjacent apartment.

The criminal had been living in the adjacent house all this time.

Homey *[Adjective]* *((of a place) pleasantly comfortable and cozy).*

We stayed at a homey bed and breakfast inn.

The room was homey and comfortable.

The restaurant has a relaxed, homey atmosphere.

Cafeteria *[Noun] (an informal restaurant in which you take the food to the table yourself and pay before eating).*

Students make lasting friendships in the cafeteria at school.

My friends and I ate in the cafeteria for lunch because they were serving pizza.

Maid *[Noun] (a woman whose job is to who clean rooms in a hotel or in someone's home).*

Her maid helped her to clean the floor.

The maid made a delicious dish yesterday.

Guesthouse *[Noun] (a private house offering accommodations that people can pay to spend the night).*

Last night, we stayed in a guesthouse.

My father bought an old guesthouse in the village where we lived.

Neighborhood *[Noun] (a particular area of a city or town where people live).*

Last night there was a big fire in the neighbourhood.

His house is the largest one in our neighborhood.

Studio flat *[Noun] (an apartment containing one main room, a kitchen, and a bathroom).*

I might just be able to afford a tiny studio flat.

We were in the living room of our studio flat.

Our studio flat is privately situated to the rear of the main house.

Furnished *[Verb]* *(containing furniture).*

They furnished their house with inexpensive furniture.

Tom's living room was tastefully furnished.

In good condition *[Expression]* *(being in a good condition, without any damage).*

The car is kept in good condition.

This bike is second-hand but it's still in good condition.

Clean and tidy *[Expression]* *(neatly and not dirty).*

The cottage was clean and tidy.

Everything was clean and tidy when I got home.

Leisure centre *[Noun]* *(a large building containing a swimming pool and other places for exercising and playing different sports).*

We went into their local leisure centre to use the swimming pool.

Our leisure centre is open seven days a week.

Exercise machines *[Noun]* *(any machine used for physical exercise or training).*

There are a lot of types of exercise machines for home you can purchase.

Exercise machines can provide strength training.

FAMILY, PEOPLE AND RELATIONSHIPS

Reunion *[Noun]* *(a social event for a group of people gather together again after not having seen each other for a long time).*

My family reunion this summer is less than one day.

The family reunion picture.

The family reunion dinner.

The month for the class reunion came, and all the members were excited.

Role model *[Noun]* *(a person who is looked up to and imitated by someone else).*

My father is the most important role model for me and my brothers.

He is my role model because he works hard; he is respectful, and he is a caring person.

Grown-up *[Adjective]* *(if someone is grown-up, he/she has reached the age of maturity).*

He has a grown-up daughter who works in a bank.

The little girl was talking to me like a grown-up lady.

Tween *[Noun]* *(a child between the ages of 10 and 12, but he/she is not yet considered a teenager).*

She has a class full of crazy tweens!

She is finding crafts for her tweens.

Meet up *[Verb]* *(to meet someone, usually by making an appointment with them first).*

After work, we all met up at the BBQ restaurant.

After school, we met up at the coffee house across the street.

Get-together *[Noun]* *(an informal social gathering in which people meet each other; reunion).*

We usually have a family get-together at Christmas.

Hold conversations *[Verb]* *(to have conversations).*

Students who are at an intermediate level should be able to hold conversations on a variety of topics in English.

Rather than just talking to people you know, you should be able to hold conversations with new people.

Relatives *[Noun]* *(the members of your family, such as an aunt, uncle, cousin, and so on).*

I have relatives in Boston.

We rarely visit our relatives.

Loved ones *[Noun]* *(people that you love, usually members of your family).*

After the accident, hundreds of people phoned the emergency helpline to know if their loved ones were alive.

People scatter ashes of their loved ones at amusement parks.

Affection [Noun] *(a gentle feeling of liking or loving someone or something).*

He had a deep affection for his parents.

Children need lots of love and affection.

Come up to me *[Verb]* *(to approach someone).*

An old man came up to me and asked for $10.

I came up to him and asked him for a light. Unfortunately, he doesn't smoke.

Calm someone down *[Verb]* *(to make someone less angry).*

I set the table and calmed him down about the sauce.

She was smiling at me, a smile which calmed me down instantly.

Talking to him calmed me down.

Optimistic *[Adjective]* *(be positive, confident and hopeful about the future or the success of something).*

He was optimistic about the outcome of the operation.

We are optimistic about the future of the company.

Break up *[Verb]* *(to end a relationship).*

He moved away after the break-up of his marriage.

She wants to break up with him.

Cheryl and her boyfriend decided to break up.

Look at/on the bright side *[Expression]* *(to think of the advantageous/positive/good things).*

I always try to look at the bright side of every situation.

Take a look at the bright side of education.

Pessimistic *[Adjective]* *(to think of the disadvantageous/negative/bad things).*

He's pessimistic about his chances of finding a good job.

Not everyone is so pessimistic about the future.

Keep in touch *[Expression]* *(to maintain communications (talking or writing) with someone).*

Let's keep in touch with each other.

We keep in touch with each other by email/writing letters.

To be around the same age *[Expression]* *(describing a group of people who have similar ages).*

We are around the same age.

My buddies Tom and Jerry are around the same age as me.

Saxophonist *[Noun]* *(someone who plays the saxophone).*

John Coltrane is supposed to be the greatest jazz saxophonist of all time.

Her father is a saxophonist, and her mother is a pianist.

Extended family *[Noun]* *(a family unit including grandparents, parents, children, aunts, uncles, and other relatives).*

She went to her boyfriend's hometown to meet his extended family.

I have been grown up in an extended family.

The in-laws *[Noun]* *(the parents and relatives of your husband or wife).*

My in-laws will be coming to visit me this weekend.

She got married and moved to her in-laws.

A family gathering *[Noun]* *(an occasion when all family members meet together for a particular purpose).*

He doesn't enjoy family gatherings very much.

During the family's gatherings in the evenings, she would sing, as she had a beautiful voice.

I see my cousins only at occasional family gatherings.

Acquaintance *[Noun]* *(a person you know a little, but is not a close friend).*

She is an old acquaintance of mine.

She's not a casual acquaintance whom you barely know.

Fall out with *[Expression]* *(to have an argument with someone).*

I had a fall out with my mom about her losing my earrings.

If she does not stop gossiping, all her friends are going to fall out with her.

Cheer sb up *[Expression]* *(to make someone feel happier).*

We tried to cheer him up.

I decided to try to cheer her up by sending her a bouquet of flowers.

He tried to cheer her up, but failed miserably.

Count on *[Verb]* *(to depend on someone to do what you want).*

She is very busy, don't count on her assistance.

You cannot count on him because he's too irresponsible.

Hang around *[Verb]* *(to spend time in a place, usually for no particular reason).*

I will just hang around here for a while.

He used to skip lessons and hang around the harbor with some other boys.

Befriend *[Verb]* *(become a friend of someone).*

We are willing to befriend the weak and the poor.

After the fight, he wanted to befriend her.

Healthy relationship *[Noun]* *(good relationship).*

It's very likely he is in a healthy relationship.

A healthy relationship should bring more happiness than stress into someone's life.

Low-income people *[Noun]* *(poor people).*

Low-income people use less dental care than high-income people.

A lot of low-income people are used to highly processed foods.

In an attempt to *[Expression]* *(in hopes of, in trying to).*

I often read fiction in an attempt to gain insights into the human experience.

Stranger *[Noun] (a person you do not know/ you have never met before).*

She treats me as if I were a stranger.

Tom is seldom at ease with strangers.

Have somebody over *[Expression] (to invite someone to come to your house for a meal, drink).*

I had some friends over for dinner last night.

I had him over for dinner a couple of times, but he never invited me back.

Creative *[Adjective] (to make or think of new and effective ideas to create something).*

He doesn't think he's as creative as she is.

He tried to find a creative way to tell her that he loved her.

My father is a very creative person.

Express oneself *[Verb] (to show your thoughts and feelings).*

She has a hard time expressing herself.

I find it difficult to express myself in Japanese.

Conservative *[Adjective] (do not like to change or accept new ideas).*

I think her father is conservative.

Tom used to be conservative.

Old people are usually more conservative than young people.

Satisfying *[Adjective] (to fulfill your desires, expectations, or needs).*

We had a very satisfying lunch at the restaurant.

Taking photographs can be a very satisfying way of capturing.

Patient *[Adjective] (to be able to wait someone or something for a long time without becoming angry or upset).*

He is a very patient man.

I have learned to be patient from my father.

Intriguing *[Adjective] (to be very interesting/ fascinating).*

I find him intriguing.

The movie looks intriguing so I'm definitely going to see it.

Come over *[Adjective] (to come to someone's house to visit for a short time).*

Would you like to come over to my house for dinner?

I came over to his house to help him with his homework.

To see eye to eye *[Expression] (to agree with someone about something).*

She doesn't always see eye to eye with her father.

We don't see eye to eye on business issues.

Caretaker *[Noun] (a person whose job is to take care of buildings while the owner is not there).*

His family hired a caretaker to maintain his summer home in London.

The caretaker is responsible for the maintenance of the office building.

Volunteer *[Noun] (to do something willingly and without being paid for it).*

Tom volunteered to help raise money for a new orphanage.

She doesn't have much time for volunteer work.

Couch potato *[Noun] (somebody who is lazy and inactive).*

He is a great couch potato; he can watch TV 24 hours a day.

Since Mary lost her job, she has become a couch potato.

Well-respected *[Adjective] (highly regarded or admired).*

His father is very well respected in the business world.

Peter seems to be a well-respected man.

Brilliant white *[Adjective]* *(very white, extremely white).*

The feathers are so brilliant white.

Self-conscious *[Adjective]* *(to be nervous, embarrassed or uncomfortable).*

I am always self-conscious on first dates.

He seemed very self-conscious when it was his turn to introduce himself to the class.

Beer belly *[Noun]* *(a fat stomach caused by drinking too much beer for a long time).*

He's only eighteen but he's already got a beer belly.

Tom is short and fat, with a large beer belly.

Bravery *[Noun]* *(courageous behaviour or actions (the will to do things that are dangerous, difficult)).*

He received an award for bravery from the police service.

I admire your bravery. **Harmony [n]:** a state of peaceful existence and agreement.

The harmony between her and her husband grew closer and closer.

Best friends are usually in harmony most of the time.

To sympathize *[Verb]* *(to show that you understand and feel sorry for someone who is in a bad situation).*

It's difficult to sympathize with a negative person who will do nothing to help himself.

I find it very hard to sympathize with him.

Conventionally *[Adverb]* *(in a traditional way).*

He is a gregarious person but not a conventionally social one.

Motivational *[Adjective] (making someone want to do something).*

His father motivational words helped him to break a record in IAS exam.

Her motivational support and inspiration have forever enriched our lives.

Exemplary *[Adjective] (providing a good example for someone to copy).*

Mary is an exemplary student who gets straight A's every term.

He is an exemplary employee, we should all study him.

Moral *[Adjective] (concerned with principles and beliefs of right and wrong behavior).*

He came with his friend for moral support.

Proper punishment by parents will teach children moral lessons.

Thoroughly *[Adverb] (completely and carefully).*

We thoroughly enjoyed the delicious meal.

He was thoroughly depressed.

Unconditional *[Adjective] (without any conditions; not limited by conditions).*

The mother's love for her daughter was unconditional.

Restless *[Adjective] (unable to rest or relax because you are bored or anxious).*

He looks like a restless man.

Children are often impatient and restless.

Pop up *[Verb] (to appear or happen in a place or situation suddenly or unexpectedly).*

Tom pops up with a white handkerchief in one hand.

She pops up in newspapers and on TV with an attractive young man.

Affectionate *[Adjective] (showing feelings of liking, warm regard or love for someone or something).*

My father is very affectionate to me.

She is very affectionate towards her children.

Crave *[Verb] (to have a very strong desire for something)*.

He craves for chocolate.

The thirsty man craved water.

Reflection *[Noun] (serious and careful thought)*.

She had no time for reflection.

After 20 years as a judge, his reflections on justice were well worth listening to.

Acceptably *[Adverb] (in a way that can be accepted)*.

He has performed acceptably without having to think.

Her communication skills are acceptably good.

Imperative *[Adjective] (extremely important or necessary)*.

It was imperative that he acts as naturally as possible.

It was imperative to destroy the bridge.

Bring up your offspring *[Expression] (to raise your children (to educate, nurture your children))*.

They are bringing up their offspring in a very strict household.

She learnt from nature and observed how animals brought up their offspring.

Generation gap *[Noun] (the difference in attitude, experiences, opinions, habits, and behaviour between young and older people that causes a lack of understanding each other)*.

They are trying to bridge the generation gap with their children.

She feels that the generation gap she has with her mother is doubly big.

Scriptwriter *[Noun] (a person who writes scripts for films/movies)*.

Her father is a scriptwriter.

The scriptwriter helped him to adapt his novel for the screen.

Dialogue *[Noun] (conversations between two or more people).*

The dialogues in romantic films are usually longer than the dialogues in action films.

The teacher asked the students to practice the dialogue in pairs.

Admirable *[Adjective] (deserving respect (someone who has qualities that you respect)).*

His devotion to your job is admirable.

My brother is admirable because he never failed me in a time of need.

Convincing *[Adjective] (that makes somebody believe that something is true or real).*

I found his argument pretty convincing.

The end of the film wasn't very convincing.

Kind-hearted *[Adjective] (to be kind, merciful and generous to other people).*

She was a warm, generous and kind-hearted woman.

He's really kind-hearted. He'll do anything to help anyone.

Give and take *[Expression] (the act of giving and receiving).*

You have to learn to give and take in any relationship.

He is taught to learn to give and take.

Lend someone a hand *[Expression] (to help somebody with something).*

We should lend her a hand when she is in trouble.

If I were in your place, I would lend him a hand.

(To) instill *[Verb] (to put a feeling, idea, or attitude gradually into someone's mind).*

The woman instilled confidence in her daughter.

The man instilled moral values in his son.

Genuine *[Adjective] (sincere and honest; authentic)*.

He was surprised to see a genuine smile on her face.

The interior of the car is covered in genuine leather.

Alienate *[Adjective] (to make someone feel isolated less friendly or sympathetic towards you)*.

His behavior alienated his friends.

She alienated her friends when she became fanatically religious.

Empathize with *[Adjective] (to understand the feeling and experience of another person)*.

It was impossible to empathize with him.

They find it difficult to empathize with others.

Benevolent *[Adjective] (kind, helpful and generous)*.

Her mother was a benevolent woman, she volunteered all of her free time to charitable organizations.

The teacher was benevolent to the student.

Goodwill *[Noun] (a friendly, kind or helpful attitude towards other people)*.

His heart is full of goodwill to all men.

A spirit of goodwill was spread in the whole community by the visit of the President.

To lift one's spirits *[Expression] (to make someone more cheerful)*.

This training has lifted our spirits, and we are motivated again.

Her telephone call really lifted his spirits.

Harshness *[Noun] (the quality of being cruel, unkind, and severe)*.

He is accused of harshness to kids that were placed under his care.

They weren't aware of the harshness of their condition.

To weigh on *[Verb]* *(to make somebody sad, anxious or worried).*

The words made her smile but weighed on him.

The failure weighed on him.

Carefree *[Adjective]* *(having no worries, anxiety or responsibilities).*

Instead of worrying, the carefree man drank his problems away.

In fact, she is a very funny and carefree person.

(To) have high hopes *[Expression]* *(to believe that something will be successful or will happen).*

He has high hopes of winning the long jump ending next month.

They have high hopes for a change in the island.

Expectation *[Noun]* *(a strong belief that something good will happen).*

As per my expectation, he completed the task on time.

The beauties of the West Lake in spring were beyond her expectation.

(To) appeal to sb/sth *[Verb]* *(to attract or interest someone or something).*

That kind of story appeals to me.

The ads appeal to consumers' need.

(To) preserve *[Verb]* *(to keep something in its original quality, feature, etc).*

Rare animals should be preserved.

Good traditions should be preserved.

Dominant *[Adjective]* *(more important, powerful or noticeable than anything else).*

The company has achieved a dominant position in the world market.

My mother was a dominant force in our family.

(To) terminate *[Verb]* *(to end or stop).*

This train will terminate at the next stop.

The countries terminated friendly relations.

(To) accomplish *[Verb]* *(to succeed in doing something; to achieve or complete something successfully).*

He accomplished his mission.

Today she is an accomplished performer.

Have a great influence on sth/sb *[Expression]* *(have a great impact on sth/sb).*

Social media has a great influence on people nowadays.

She was a kind woman and had a great influence on me.

Her stories had a great influence on me.

Well-known *[Adjective]* *(widely known about by many people; famous).*

Her books are well known. You can find them in any bookshop in the city.

His father is a well-known lawyer.

Piece of advice *[Noun]* *(a suggestion about what somebody should do in a particular situation).*

He gave me a piece of advice yesterday.

Her father gave her a piece of good advice.

Approachable *[Adjective]* *(friendly and easy to meet or talk to).*

Her father is very kind and approachable.

She can talk to her boss about any problems she has because he is very approachable.

Sufficient *[Adjective] (enough; adequate).*

His efforts were not sufficient to earn him victory.

The budget is not sufficient to cover everything that needs doing.

Upper class *[Noun] (a group of people who have the highest social rank and wealth).*

They came from wealthy, upper-class families.

He belongs to the rich American upper class.

To plead *[Verb] (to beg, or ask for something in a serious and emotional way).*

She pleaded with her mother to let her go to the party.

He pleaded innocent to the charges.

Wrongdoing *[Noun] (an illegal or dishonest behavior).*

He was guilty of some wrongdoing.

He has strenuously denied any criminal wrongdoing.

Needless to say = it goes without saying that *[Expression] (obviously).*

Needless to say, we were so excited about the journey.

It goes without saying that they are very happy about the new baby.

Significance *[Noun] (importance).*

His war medal has a special significance for his family.

She felt she could not grasp its significance.

To be an inspiration to *[Expression] (to make somebody excited about something).*

His courage is an inspiration to us all.

She was an inspiration to everyone who knew her.

Their father was an inspiration to the whole family.

Sleep soundly *[Expression]* *(sleep very well).*

You will sleep soundly if you get plenty of exercise during the day.

The baby was sleeping soundly in her mother's arms.

I slept soundly last night.

Courteous *[Noun]* *(to be polite, especially in a formal way).*

It was courteous of him to write a letter of thanks.

Mary was very courteous to us.

Ill-mannered *[Adjective]* *(rude; impolite).*

His ill-mannered behaviour irritated me.

The teacher has punished Tom because he was ill-mannered.

Negligence *[Noun]* *(failure to give someone/something proper care or attention).*

She will be paid off for her negligence.

His negligence could let his son become infected now.

Disrespect *[Noun]* *(a lack of respect for someone/something).*

Some students disrespect teachers and parents.

He felt she had total disrespect for men.

To bond with somebody *[Expression]* *(to develop or create a strong relationship or trust with somebody).*

She has a special bond with her brother because they grew up together, have many memories and share many secrets.

Cultural events and activities will help people to bond with each other.

Enthusiastic *[Adjective]* *(feeling or showing a lot of excitement and interest about somebody/something).*

He seems very enthusiastic about his role in the play.

Mary is very enthusiastic about her new job.

(To) aspire to *[Verb]* *(to have a strong desire to achieve something).*

After watching the professional baseball game, Tom aspired to become a famous athlete one day.

She aspires to become a teacher.

Proficiency *[Noun]* *(the ability to do something well because of advancement in knowledge, experience or skill).*

The test results were used as an index of language proficiency.

Sarah has a high level of oral proficiency in Japanese.

Lift one's spirits *[Expression]* *(to make somebody feel cheerful).*

The rising of the sun always lifts my spirits.

Listening to upbeat songs lifts his spirits.

To come highly recommended *[Expression]* *(to say that something is really good, and suggest people for a particular purpose).*

The local restaurant comes highly recommended.

The play with such true witticisms and parables comes highly recommended.

Freelancer *[Noun]* *(someone who is self-employed instead of being a company employee).*

He worked mainly as a freelancer.

I am looking for a dedicated freelancer who is willing to work full time.

To drift apart *[Verb]* *(to gradually become less friendly or intimate).*

Over the years his college friends and he have drifted apart.

The two girls, who had been friends since school, drifted apart after they started work.

Idolise *[Verb] (to admire and respect somebody very much).*

He was idolized by movie fans all over the world.

She idolizes her big brother, who is a professional footballer.

Celebrity *[Noun] (someone who is famous, especially in the entertainment business or sport).*

He achieved celebrity status after filming this movie.

He is a celebrity who keeps his simplicity and his privacy.

Innate *[Adjective] (inborn; natural).*

He seldom stopped smiling and never lost his innate sense of fun.

Inspire *[Verb] (to make someone feel that they are eager to do something and can do it).*

His courage inspired his followers.

They are inspired to live their purpose with passion!

The basketball star said he was inspired to follow in the footsteps of his father.

Outlook *[Noun] (a person's point of view about something).*

She really changed her outlook on life after having a heart attack.

Many women have a negative outlook on marriage.

Personable *[Adjective] (if you are personal, you look attractive to other people because you have a pleasant appearance or character).*

He's strong-willed but very personable.

She's a very personable, intelligent lady.

To reunite *[Verb] (to bring people together again after a period of separation).*

The police reunited him with his son after a long absence in Japan.

They were reunited after a separation of more than 10 years.

Head over heels in love *[Expression] (in love with someone (loving someone very much)).*

David and Lucy are head over heels in love with each other and are going to get married next week.

She soon found herself head over heels in love with this man.

My father fell head over heels in love with my mom the first time he talked to her.

To tie the knot *[Expression] (to get married).*

Bill and Sarah will tie the knot next month.

After 3 years of dating each other, Tom and Mary have finally decided to tie the knot next July.

Have ups and downs *[Expression] (if someone has ups and downs, they experience a mixture of good things and bad things.)*

I have encountered with ups and downs in my life.

The relationship between Peter and Joe has had a lot of ups and downs.

To endear oneself to someone *[Expression] (to make someone liked by someone else).*

Reducing salaries is not a way for a boss to endear himself to his employees.

He managed to endear himself to my entire family.

He tried to endear himself to her with flowers and chocolate.

To entice *[Verb] (to persuade someone to do something by offering them pleasure, reward or*

My brother was enticed by the smell of coffee in the doorway he found at a nearby shop.

My mom was enticed into buying things she doesn't really want by the adverts.

To derive *[Verb] (to get or obtain something from something else).*

I will not purchase these supplements because I am not sure I will derive any benefit from their use.

I derived great pleasure from reading your book.

He derived great pleasure from taking us on his journeys.

To make small talk *[Expression] (to make a polite conversation about unimportant things such as the weather).*

He was never very good at making small talk with her parents.

We made small talk for half an hour.

To be wary of *[Expression] (not completely trusting something; watchful, cautious, or alert).*

We must teach children to be wary of strangers.

Be wary of the roads; they're slippery.

(To) float on air *[Expression] (to feel extremely happy).*

Tom was floating on air after he won first prize.

On their wedding day, most couples feel like they are floating on air.

Beyond one's expectation *[Expression] (greater than what was expected).*

The demand to learn Mandarin overseas is beyond our expectation.

The final verdict was death, which was completely beyond our expectation.

To be in the peak of the condition *[Expression] (to be in the best possible physical condition; to be very fit).*

He is fit, strong and in the peak of condition.

Athletes must be in the peak of condition to win.

To offer emotional support *[Expression] (to give counselling or encouragement to a person who is suffering from a mental health problem or stress).*

They can offer emotional support and information.

Families and friends can offer emotional support, especially at key times.

A dual-income family *[Noun] (a family that gets money from two separate incomes from the father and mother).*

One of the many benefits of having a spouse is the ability to leverage being a dual income family to pay off debt and save money.

Newcomer *[Noun] (a person who has recently arrived in a place).*

Australia is a friendly country, where newcomers and older residents mix well.

Canadian winter weather poses a number of challenges for newcomers from tropical climates.

Fulfill one's dream *[Expression] (to do or to achieve what someone hoped to do).*

He started to make plans to fulfill his dreams.

She tried to get an education so that she could fulfill her dreams.

Potential *[Noun] (qualities that exist and can be developed or achieved).*

His company has a lot of potential for future growth.

He has a lot of talent, but he hasn't really fulfilled his potential.

Skillset *[Noun] (a person's range of skills or abilities that he/she has developed).*

If you want to be an accountant, your skill set must include an ability to understand mathematics.

Hard skills represent the required skill set for the specific job.

To carry out *[Verb] (to perform; to do a particular piece of work).*

He has the ability to carry out big plans.

Although in poor health, she continued to carry out her duties.

Look up to *[Verb] (to admire and respect someone).*

We look up to him as a hero.

Children should look up to their parents.

She wants him to look up to her as a hard worker.

Admirable *[Adjective] (having qualities that you admire and respect).*

His dedication to her studies is admirable.

He is an admirable man who has won numerous medals of valor.

The construction of the roof is particularly admirable.

Charitable *[Adjective] (concerned with charities or helping the poor or people who are in need).*

She performs charitable work to help the poor.

He has tried to be charitable about his sister's problems.

Reach the top *[Expression] (become very successful at something).*

This book is about successful business people and how they reached the top.

Like all great movie actors, Tom Hanks trained for years until he reached the top.

Performance-enhancing *[Adjective] (things - such as drugs - that people take illegally to make them better or more successful in a sports competition).*

He was banned from competition for two years after admitting he had used performance-enhancing drugs.

Performance-enhancing drugs are a bad thing for several reasons.

Sensitive *[Adjective]* *(to be able to understand other people's needs, emotions and feelings).*

I'm very sensitive to the cold, so I think I'd better put on a sweater.

She works in a home for old people, and she is very kind and sensitive.

She's very sensitive to criticism of her children.

Be prone to *[Adjective]* *(likely to suffer from something unpleasant or regrettable (an illness, etc.))*

She is prone to lose her temper when people disagree with her.

Farmed fish are prone to disease.

Worthy *[Adjective]* *(having good qualities that deserve your respect, admiration, or support).*

His behavior is worthy of praise.

Her behavior is worthy of respect.

Mentor *[Noun]* *(an experienced and trusted adviser who gives someone younger or with less experience help and advice over a period of time).*

After college, my professor became my close friend and mentor.

My brother needed a mentor to teach him about the world of politics.

Lack of respect for *[Expression]* *(to have no special regard or respect for someone or something).*

He has a lack of respect for women.

Lack of respect for elders is growing.

Depression *[Noun]* *(feeling very sad or anxious; having a depressed mood).*

She suffered from depression after losing her job.

His depression made him unable to get out of bed.

Generation gap *[Noun] (the difference in attitude, experiences, opinions, habits, and behaviour between young and older people that causes a lack of understanding each other.)*

I was aware of a real generation gap between us.

The film also highlights the generation gap but in a light comedy manner.

Traditionalist *[Noun] (a person who believes in and follows the old, traditional ideas).*

Some traditionalists think that a woman should look after the home and not go out to work.

Traditionalists are people who were born before 1946.

Nuclear family *[Noun] (a family that consists of parents and children).*

The nuclear family makes better communication possible between parents and children.

In modern times, the most common family structure is the nuclear family.

Working parents *[Noun] (parents who both engages in a work life (go out to work)).*

While their children are at nursery school, Peter works as an engineer and Mary is a teacher. They are working parents.

Many working parents spend up to a quarter of their income on childcare.

Double income *[Noun] (two salaries).*

Parents of small families with a double income can invest more in the education and well-being of their children.

As Tom and Mary both earn salaries, they can afford to buy more things for their home as a result of the family's double income.

Realistic *[Adjective] (showing a sensible and practical idea of what can be achieved).*

He is realistic enough to know that it won't work.

The man was realistic about what his circumstances were.

Underestimate *[Verb] (to estimate something at too low a value, rate, or less important than it actually is).*

Her determination to pass the exam should not be underestimated.

His talent has always been underestimated.

Never underestimate your power to change yourself!

Hardship *[Noun] (a situation in which your life is difficult or unpleasant, often because you do not have enough money, clothes or food).*

We have to endure a lot of hardships in life.

She has suffered many hardships.

A win-win situation *[Noun] (a situation in which the result is good for everyone who is involved in).*

The idea in a win-win situation is that nobody loses.

UK and China collaboration is a win-win situation for both countries.

Embark on *[Verb] (start to do something new, important or difficult).*

He is about to embark on a new career as a doctor.

She was now ready to embark on her journey of adventure.

Family ties *[Noun] (family links or connections).*

She decided not to take a new job in London because her family ties in Japan were too strong.

Obviously, she thought family ties were more important than education.

Working mothers *[Noun] (women who work outside the home and also have to take care of their children at home).*

There can be both negative and positive effects of working mothers on their children.

Working mothers admit starting a family set back their careers.

Ties of kinship *[Noun] (the fact of being related to the link or the relationship between members of the same family).*

This was not just a friendly greeting but a formal recognition of the ties of kinship between them.

In the modern world, people are always moving to a new place to live, and this has weakened traditional ties of kinship.

Show off *[Verb] (to intentionally act in a way to attract other people's attention or admiration).*

She likes to wear short skirts to show off her legs.

She did a quick twirl to show off her dress.

Mind *[Verb] (to care about, feel annoyed, or unhappy about something).*

I don't mind if she is sociable or not.

Don't mind Lucy; she likes to sing in the mornings!

Appreciate *[Verb] (to recognise or understand that something is valuable or important).*

You talk to me, and try to cheer me up, and I really appreciate it.

I would appreciate it if you would deal with this matter urgently.

Contact *[Verb] (to communicate with someone either by talking or writing).*

Tom wasn't able to contact Mary by phone.

We will contact you as soon as we know.

Bear *[Verb] (to accept, endure or tolerate something unpleasant).*

She can't bear the taste of bananas.

He could hardly bear the pain.

I can't bear to be doing nothing!

Be madly in love with *[Expression]* *(to love someone very much in a romantic way).*

He was madly in love with her.

There is no secret left in the fact that she is madly in love with him.

Interpersonal relationships *[Noun]* *(a strong bond between 2 or more people).*

Interpersonal relationship skill is so important for your career advancement.

The interpersonal relationship is a solid, deep-rooted and joined between two or more people.

Well-being *[Noun]* *(the state of being comfortable, healthy, happy or prosperous).*

Sleep is necessary for your overall health, fitness and mental well-being.

All people desire an increase in well-being.

Nurture *[Verb]* *(to take care of, feed, and protect someone or something while they are growing).*

Teachers should nurture their students' creativity.

Good parents nurture their children so they will become happy and healthy adults.

If your brother wants to become a great dancer, he should nurture his talent by practicing every day.

Longevity *[Noun]* *(living for a long time; lasting a long time).*

If he quits smoking, he will increase the longevity of his life.

I wish you longevity and health.

Single-parent family *[Noun]* *(someone who brings up a child or children alone, without a partner).*

He comes from a single-parent family, and he is a single child.

The child is raised in a single-parent family.

Paternal *[Adjective]* *(relating to a father)*.

Her paternal grandfather served in World War II.

He visits his paternal grandmother every summer.

Maternal *[Adjective]* *(relating to a mother)*.

When I visit my maternal uncle, he always tells me stories about my mother.

His maternal grandmother gave him a digital watch for his birthday.

In-laws *[Noun]* *(people who you are related to by marriage, especially parents and close relatives of your husband or wife)*.

There's no love lost between her and her in-laws.

All my in-laws live far away.

Adorable *[Adjective]* *(very attractive; delightful; charming)*.

Her smile looks adorable.

Oh, your baby is adorable!

What an adorable child!

Understanding and caring *[Expression]* *(a feeling of sympathy for someone else who is suffering problems that have caused unhappiness)*.

We need to start with understanding and caring for people around the globe.

Make time for listening, and providing understanding and caring communication.

They seem warm, understanding and caring.

Sibling *[Noun]* *(your brothers and sisters)*.

Tom and Lucy are siblings.

They are siblings, but they only lived together for a few years.

Adolescence *[Noun] (the period of time when a person changes from being a child to being a young adult).*

Adolescence is the period of progression from childhood to adulthood.

Many bodily changes occur during adolescence.

Conflict *[Noun] (a serious disagreement or argument between people or groups).*

Whatever the issue was, the conflict between Alex and Dulce remained.

His boss and he disagreed over paid time off, and now there is a conflict between them which causes tension in the office.

The external conflict between parents and children.

Upbringing *[Noun] (the way that parents care for their children and teach them to behave when they are growing up).*

My wife's upbringing was completely different from mine.

The children had had a harsh upbringing.

I wonder what it was about his upbringing that made him so insecure.

Build a relationship = develop a relationship = establish a relationship = form a relationship = have a relationship.

The best way to build a relationship is to listen, learn, and ask questions.

I wanted to develop a relationship with my team.

The manager tried to establish a good relationship of trust with his employees.

They form a relationship based on love and shared beliefs.

I think they have a relationship!

A close relationship *[Noun] (a relationship that is connected by shared interests and shared feelings).*

Tom has a close relationship with Mary.

She has a close relationship with her siblings.

A long-standing relationship *[Noun] (a relationship that has existed or continued for a long time).*

Tom had a long-standing relationship with Lucy.

We are pleased to have a long-standing relationship with our client.

To take after somebody *[Expression] (to be similar in appearance or character to someone in your family).*

Her daughter doesn't take after her at all.

That boy takes after his father.

Foster family *[Noun] (a family that takes care of or bring up children whose parents are dead or unable to look after them).*

The number of children living with a foster family is limited to six.

There are many children waiting to be part of a foster family.

LAW, CRIME AND PUNISHMENT

Disqualified *[Adjective] (to stop somebody from doing something because they have done something wrong).*

He had been drinking and driving and he was disqualified from driving for six months.

She was disqualified from a competition when she refused to empty her pockets after a letter disappeared.

Enact *[Verb] (to make into law; to put a law into practice).*

The law was finally enacted today.

The state death penalty law was enacted in 1972.

Comes into play *[Expression] (come into effect; come into action).*

The law on sentencing came into play.

Heavily fine *[Noun] (to charge someone a lot of money since he/she has violated a law or regulation).*

He was heavily fined for speeding.

The company was heavily fined for polluting the river's water.

He was not only thrown into jail but also heavily fined.

Consequently *[Adverb] (as a result; therefore (used to say something that happens because of something else)).*

He didn't like the cake; consequently, he threw it all away.

Sarah decided not to use a map; consequently, she got lost and never found her way out of the forest.

He didn't study for his test; consequently, he failed.

Legalize *[Verb] (to make something become legal).*

The government won't ever legalize the drugs trade.

Solid evidence *[Noun] (very convincing evidence).*

He's not worried because he has a solid evidence.

There is reasonably solid evidence against him.

Taken into consideration *[Expression] (take a look or take into account or consider).*

The judge took into consideration the fact that it was her first offense.

The judge took into consideration that he used no violence in the commission of his crime.

Confine *[Verb] (restrict/limit).*

Why do you confine me?

Is it cruel to confine a bird in a cage?

Comply with *[Verb] (follow/abide by).*

He failed to comply with the requirements of noncustodial sentences.

All employees in the company must comply with our guidelines.

The crime rate *[Noun] (the ratio of crimes in a particular area during a period of time).*

The crime rate is decreasing in Canada.

This country has the fastest-growing crime rate in the world.

As a result of more unemployment, the crime rate in the area is increasing.

Offenders *[Noun] (people who commit crimes/ illegal acts).*

The number of offenders has climbed in many countries over recent decades.

The more laws, the more offenders.

Commit a crime *[Verb] (to do something wrong or illegal).*

A person who commits a crime is a criminal.

He committed a terrible crime.

Copyright *[Noun] (refers to the legal right of the owner of the intellectual property).*

Those people who use copyright material without the permission of the author will be fined.

Release *[Verb] (to set free from prison).*

He was sentenced to 7 years in prison, but was released after 5 years for good behavior.

Some prisoners who are sentenced to jail for life will never be released.

Obligations *[Noun] (things which you must do because it is your duty or commitment).*

If you have an obligation to do something, it is your duty to do that thing.

We have a legal obligation to pay our taxes.

Tom didn't fulfill his obligations.

Homeless *[Adjective] ((of a person) having no home).*

We're having a lottery to raise money for homeless families.

There is an increasing number of homeless people living in our city.

Easy money *[Noun] (money that's made without working hard, and sometimes dishonestly earned).*

He started stealing as a way of making easy money.

Some criminals steal from banks or houses as a way to make easy money.

Break the law *[Verb] (to fail to obey a law; to act contrary to a law; to do something illegal.)*

Doctors who break the law face up to two years in prison.

Tom didn't break any laws.

Unregulated *[Adjective] (not controlled or supervised by laws or rules).*

As a result of unregulated fishing, there are now almost no fish in that part of the ocean.

Unregulated use of the islands in the study area could result in minor or moderate impacts to wildlife.

To enforce strict regulations on *[Expression] (to make sure a tough punishment to people if they do something against the laws or regulations).*

Due to the high-quality requirements on medical systems, regulatory bodies enforce strict regulations on how products are created.

The police had to enforce strict regulations on the people so that they would stop polluting the river.

Obligatory *[Adjective] (compulsory; something that you must do because of the rules or the law).*

It is obligatory for us to obey the laws.

In low-rise buildings, the use of the stairs should be obligatory.

Burglary *[Adjective] (the act of entering a building illegally and stealing things from it).*

He had been caught in committing burglary and forgery.

He is serving a three-year sentence for burglary.

Insecurity *[Noun] (the state of not being safe or protected).*

Due to his insecurity, he always felt that others were making fun of him.

Adolescence is often a period of insecurity.

Surveillance cameras *[Noun] (video cameras used for the purpose of observing an area where a crime may be committed).*

In terms of greater security on the roads, more surveillance cameras should be installed.

Outside the bank, the security company installed surveillance cameras to deter any potential robbers.

Drug trafficking *[Noun]* *(trading drugs illegally)*.

The police arrested the man for drug trafficking.

She had been making out with a man who might be involved in drug trafficking.

Consequently *[Adverb]* *(as a result; therefore (used to say something that happens because of something else))*.

She didn't like the pudding; consequently, she threw it all away.

Tom decided not to use a map; consequently, he got lost and never found his way out of the forest.

He didn't study for his test; consequently, he failed.

Address *[Verb]* *(to try to deal with a problem)*.

The problems created by traffic pollution must be addressed urgently.

Social problems must be addressed by community networks.

Compulsion *[Noun]* *(the state of being compelled to do something that you do not want to do)*.

The legal system is based on compulsion.

The child felt a compulsion to run as he walked past the old house.

Compel *[Verb]* *(to force someone to do something)*.

The law will compel employers to provide health insurance.

The teacher cannot compel good work from unwilling students.

Unregulated *[Adjective]* *(not controlled or supervised by laws or rules)*.

The unregulated sale of tobacco to children must be dealt with by the police.

Free enterprise is the unregulated market in which businesses are free to buy and sell.

To impose discipline *[Verb] (to make people obey the rules of a particular organization (school or college)).*

He reacted by imposing tough discipline and demanding better results.

Management imposed discipline that is too harsh.

If teachers fail to impose discipline in class, then students will not learn anything.

BUSINESS

Fast food chain *[Noun] (a network of restaurants serving fast food like McDonald's, KFC, etc).*

The McDonald's fast food chain opened hundreds of restaurants in China.

This fast food chain has become enormously successful in serving food that is relatively unhealthy.

Collective level *[Noun] (done by people acting as a group).*

This problem must be solved on a collective level, not an individual level.

Build up *[Verb] (to develop).*

It is important for companies to build up a good relationship with their clients/customers.

If you want to sell more, you have to build up a good relationship with your customers.

Indispensable *[Adjective] (absolutely necessary or essential; very important).*

His assistance is indispensable to our success.

Water is indispensable to life.

Amusement center *[Noun] (a place that has a lot of things to play for fun).*

Our city has a fantastic amusement center for children to play while their parents are shopping.

It is a fantastic amusement center called Ocean Park.

Discount coupon *[Noun] (a voucher that allows someone to pay less money than usual for an item).*

All users are given discount coupons when they finish filling out a survey.

I will send you a discount coupon so you can use on a future order with us.

Maximize customer satisfaction *[Expression] (maximize customer happiness).*

You can maximize customer satisfaction and increase revenue by delivering what is valuable to your customers.

Ideal solution *[Expression] (good solution).*

Tom came up with an ideal solution.

It seemed like a good solution.

Make it to the top *[Expression] (to be very successful).*

There is only one way to make it to the top: hard work.

It would be more difficult for each member to try to make it to the top alone.

Benefits *[Noun] (advantages or profits gained from something).*

She is currently collecting unemployment benefits.

The benefits of taking the drug outweigh its risks.

To be user-friendly *[Adjective] (to be easy to use, learn or understand without advanced skills).*

The latest version of Nokia has become more user-friendly.

The instructions are user-friendly and practical.

Beneficial *[Adjective] (helpful, useful).*

Beneficial effects of a balanced diet.

This treatment can be very beneficial, especially for old people.

Revenue *[Noun] (the amount of money which a company receives from its business).*

The company is looking for another source of revenue.

The revenue from the bond sale was used to improve several bridges in the city.

To make the most of something *[Expression] (to exploit something as much as possible)*.

He planned to make the most of his trip to England.

He made the most of his opportunity.

Reputable *[Adjective] (generally considered to be reliable, and having a good reputation)*.

My information comes from a very reputable source.

This woman is from a reputable family.

To allocate somebody something *[Expression] (to officially distribute something or someone for a particular purpose)*.

The government has refused to allocate the funds needed to hire more teachers.

The company director wants to allocate additional staff to the marketing department.

A lavish amount of something *[Noun] (a huge amount of something)*.

There was a lavish amount of food and drinks set upon the table.

We spent a lavish amount of money on our trip last month.

(To) upgrade *[Verb] (to improve something so that it would be more powerful, efficient, better, etc)*.

The funds will be used to upgrade and repair the building.

They upgraded the hotel to attract more business people.

Adjustment *[Noun] (a small change to make something better)*.

Real wages have decreased after the adjustment for inflation.

He made a quick adjustment to his new job.

(To) incorporate *[Verb] (to include something so that it forms a part of something else).*

You can incorporate this document with the others.

We have incorporated all the latest safety features into the design.

Market leader *[Noun] (a company with the largest market share in an industry or sells the largest quantity of a particular product).*

Their products have become established and their company is a market leader.

Becoming a market leader is very difficult in any kind of market conditions nowadays.

Enterprises *[Noun] (companies, businesses, corporations).*

Small enterprises are feeling the squeeze of inflation.

The Promotion Agency was established to promote social enterprises.

To generate *[Verb] (to produce or create something).*

Massive amounts of carbon dioxide are generated every day.

Nuclear power is used to generate electricity.

Charitable donations *[Noun] (money given to nonprofit organizations which help the poor or people in need of help).*

Charitable donations were made to help those who lost their homes during the flood.

The charitable donations of profits and resources given by corporations to nonprofit organizations.

Accountancy *[Noun] (the profession or work done by accountants in dealing with figures for tax or other purposes).*

She is studying accountancy.

A degree in mathematics is essential for a career in accountancy.

An entrepreneur *[Noun]* *(a person who makes profits by organizing and operating a business or businesses).*

John is an entrepreneur who built a massive company through hard work.

The entrepreneur takes business risks in the hope of making a profit.

Imbalance *[Noun]* *(the state of being out of proportion or distribution, in a way that causes problems).*

The imbalance between the import and export figures can only be solved by reducing imports.

The government must redress the imbalance in spending on black and white children.

Core values *[Noun]* *(the most important values or fundamental beliefs of something).*

Young children learn about the origins and core values of their motherland through history lessons.

The core values of the French Revolution were Liberty, Equality, and Property.

Run out *[Verb]* *(to be used up or finished; come to an end).*

She has run out of patience with him.

They have run out of ideas.

We've run out of milk.

Guarantee *[Verb]* *(a promise that something will be done or will happen).*

When you buy a car, you'll get a service guarantee.

There is no guarantee that money will bring happiness.

Renewable energy *[Noun]* *(energy from a source that is not depleted when used, such as wind or solar power so that there is no danger that it will finish).*

Wind and solar power are examples of renewable energy sources.

Technology enables us to exploit more renewable energy sources.

Contribute *[Verb] (to be one of the causes of something).*

Technology has contributed to improvements in our lives.

Her lack of exercise contributed to her heart problems.

Boundless *[Adjective] (unlimited; without limits).*

He has boundless energy and enthusiasm.

She is a woman of apparently boundless optimism.

To fund *[Verb] (to provide money for something official or for a particular purpose).*

The group funded three new scholarships.

The construction of the new bridge will be funded by the government.

The cost of the statue was funded by contributions from both the French and the Americans.

Prosperity *[Noun] (the state of being successful, especially in financial respects).*

Your prosperity or poverty is a result of your thinking.

Our future prosperity depends on economic growth.

Imbalance *[Noun] (the state or condition of lacking balance, in a way that causes problems).*

The trade imbalance is likely to rise again in 1990.

Female hormone imbalance is a major cause of infertility.

The imbalance between the import and export figures can only be solved by reducing imports.

Investing heavily *[Expression] (investing a lot of money in something).*

It is true that in many countries, governments are investing heavily in extending internet access.

Japanese automakers are investing heavily in new plant and equipment.

Counterproductive *[Adjective] (having an opposite result or effect to the result that you want or desire).*

Eating a gallon of ice cream is counterproductive to her diet.

Increases in taxation would be counterproductive.

Telemarketing *[Noun] (the activity of using the telephone to sell goods or services).*

My brother told me he was working for a telemarketing company.

Most people don't know the difference between Telemarketing and Telesales.

MONEY, SHOPPING, CLOTHES AND FASHION

Save up *[Verb]* *(to save money for future use).*

He is saving (up) for a new car.

Her boyfriend plans to save up and buy a sports car.

Budget *[Noun]* *(the amount of money that someone has available to spend).*

He is on a tight budget this month, so he can't go out to dinner with her.

She did not buy the item because it did not fit her budget.

Afford *[Verb]* *(to have enough money to buy something).*

He can't afford to buy a new car.

We can afford to go to London this summer.

Economize *[Verb]* *(to save money by spending less money than you normally do).*

He was short of money and had to economize greatly.

We plan to economize on holidays this year by camping instead of booking a hotel.

A bit pricey *[Adjective]* *(a little expensive).*

It's a bit pricey but the food is delicious.

I love this software. However, it is a bit pricey.

Affordable *[Adjective]* *(inexpensive; reasonably priced; cheap enough so that people can buy it/pay for it).*

Tom bought a repainted used car that was affordable and easy to repair.

Rolex watches are not as affordable even though they are better than Sekonda.

A change of clothes *[Noun] (an extra set of clothes that someone takes with him/her when he/she goes to stay somewhere).*

He brought a change of clothes with him to swim in the sea.

I'd bring a change of clothes including t-shirts, jeans and casual shoes.

Try clothes on *[Expression] (to put on clothes to see if they fit).*

They tried clothes on in half of the shops.

I was trying clothes on in the dressing room.

Earn *[Verb] (to obtain or receive money in return for work that you do).*

The man is not clever but he earns a lot of money.

A soccer player earns a lot of money.

To pay through the nose for something *[Expression] (to pay a large amount of money for something).*

He paid through the nose for lunch, in order to impress his wife on their anniversary.

She paid through the nose for her daughter's university tuition.

Reasonable *[Adjective] ((of prices) not too expensive, affordable).*

They are looking for a place to eat that had reasonable prices.

The restaurant serves good food at reasonable prices.

Big money *[Noun] (a large amount of money).*

He made big money big money as a spokesman for governments accused of human rights abuses.

You'll never make big money unless you work hard.

Fares *[Noun] (the money a passenger on public transportation (bus, train, taxi etc.) has to pay to travel).*

The bus fares have been raised by 10 percent.

The taxi driver picked up his fares at the airport.

A waste of money *[Expression] (to spend money in a bad way).*

Smoking is a waste of money.

Buying video games is a waste of money.

Savings: *[Noun] (money that you have saved in an account in a bank).*

They were able to retire on their savings.

He has his savings in stocks.

They put all their savings into buying a house.

Discount store *[Noun] (a store that sells goods at low prices).*

Tom is able to buy many things he needs at a local discount store.

My brother opened his first discount store in the local town.

A shopaholic *[Noun] (a person who spends too much time shopping).*

My sister is a shopaholic. She enjoys going shopping and buying things.

Sarah is such a shopaholic that she maxed out all three of her credit cards.

PERSONALITY, FEELINGS AND EMOTIONS

Panic *[Adjective]* *(a sudden feeling of fear or anxiety)*.

He was running in panic toward the building.

Tom gets in a panic whenever he has to do the test.

Sociable *[Adjective]* *(someone who is friendly and enjoys spending time with other people)*.

He is a sociable reliable man.

She is sociable, generous and very kind.

Discouraged *[Adjective]* *(feeling less enthusiastic, hopeful or confident about something)*.

She became totally discouraged after she failed her course a second time.

His parents discouraged him from playing games too much.

Hooked *[Adjective]* *(be addicted to something)*.

My neighbour is hooked on cocaine.

My cousin is hooked on smack.

My brother is hooked on football.

Ingenious *[Adjective]* *(very clever and inventive)*.

He is the most ingenious songwriter I've ever known.

An ingenious researcher can find the real ingredients of 'fake' medicine.

Hopeless *[Adjective]* *(despairing; very unhappy)*.

It's hopeless trying to convince him.

He feels hopeless about the future.

She seems to feel hopeless about recovering.

Regrettable *[Adjective] (something that makes you feel sad and sorry about).*

It is regrettable that he was not elected as the leader of the team.

Her tiredness caused her to make a regrettable error.

Warm-hearted *[Adjective] (to be friendly, kind, generous and always willing to help other people).*

He is warm-hearted and known for joking around.

My grandmother is a warm-hearted person who taught me how to love and be good with other people.

Lose one's patience *[Expression] (if you lose your patience, you are unable to keep your temper, and become suddenly annoyed angry).*

He lost his patience and hit the old man.

My mom never cursed and rarely lost her patience with us.

Tom had lost his patience with his noisy neighbors.

Amiable *[Adjective] (friendly, sociable and pleasant).*

I love going to my doctor's office because his staff is so amiable!

She is not only beautiful but also amiable to everybody.

Suspicious *[Adjective] (to show a distrust of someone or something).*

Her manner made me suspicious.

The police became suspicious about her death.

Outstanding *[Adjective] (excellent or extremely good).*

Ronaldo is an outstanding football player.

He scored outstanding marks in the exams.

Considerate *[Adjective]* *(kind and helpful (pay attention to the wishes and feelings of other people)).*

He is very considerate to his wife and her family.

Although Peter is young, he is very considerate.

Thoughtful *[Adjective]* *(showing attention or consideration for the needs and feeling of other people).*

Paul is very thoughtful and patient.

Mary is very thoughtful, so she always thinks about helping others.

Bossy *[Adjective]* *(to describe someone who is always telling other people what to do).*

We liked him a lot, even if he was bossy.

She was bossy, arrogant or narcissistic.

Officious *[Adjective]* *(to describe someone who uses their authority or position to tell people what to do).*

The receptionist was officious.

An officious man is seldom rich.

Irresponsible *[Adjective]* *(to describe someone who has no feeling of responsibility for something).*

I felt that it was irresponsible to advocate the legalization of drugs.

In my opinion, what he did was irresponsible and reckless.

To feel relieved *[Verb]* *(feeling good because a difficult problem has been solved).*

Sarah's parents felt relieved to hear that her plane was on time.

He felt relieved and a sense of peace.

Shame *[Noun] (a guilty and embarrassed feeling that you have when you or someone else has behaved badly).*

Shame *[Verb] (to make someone feel that they are guilty and embarrassed).*

The story goes that he died of shame at his failure.

There's no shame in being poor.

After a number of drugs scandals, the sport of cycling was shamed by the media.

Witty *[Adjective] (able to use words in clever and funny things).*

Our tour guide in Paris was so witty.

We laughed a lot because the actor was so witty.

Convenient *[Adjective] (to be easy, very useful or suitable for a person's needs or a particular purpose).*

My house is in a convenient location for travelling to Tokyo.

I bought this laptop for my son because it is very convenient.

Awkward *[Adjective] (uncomfortable; hard to deal with or handle).*

I felt a little awkward.

The machine is very awkward to operate.

Proficient *[Adjective] (to be very skilled or good at something).*

My brother is very proficient at computer programming.

She is a proficient, graceful swimmer.

He's proficient at his job.

Insightful *[Adjective] (having or showing a clear and deep understanding of something).*

Her comment and suggestion are very insightful.

His analysis of the problem was very insightful and everything became clear to me.

Envious *[Adjective]* *(feeling or showing envy; wanting something that somebody else has).*

He was envious of his friend's promotion.

She was envious of her sister's beauty.

(To be) grateful to *[Adjective]* *(feeling or showing an appreciation of kindness because someone has done something kind for you).*

We are extremely grateful to all the teachers for their help.

She was grateful to him for being very kind to her.

Insensitive *[Adjective]* *(showing no concern or sympathy for others' feelings).*

He's completely insensitive to her feelings.

I feel my girlfriend is very insensitive about my problem.

Enviable *[Adjective]* *(something that is so good that other people also want to have).*

He has built up an enviable reputation as a scientist.

She is a woman of enviable beauty.

Funny *[Adjective]* *(humorous (causing laughter or amusement)).*

Clowns always try to be funny.

He was very funny as a child.

The story was very funny and he kept laughing while reading it.

Humorous *[Adjective]* *(to be funny (causing laughter or amusement)).*

He was quite humorous, and I liked that about him.

That joke you just told was not as humorous as the last one.

Witty *[Adjective] (clever and funny).*

He was insightful, clever and witty.

She is honest, but at the same time is witty.

Amusing *[Adjective] (funny or entertaining (causing laughter or providing entertainment)).*

I found Tom quite amusing.

He always exaggerates to make his stories more amusing.

Shy *[Adjective] (being reserved, nervous and embarrassed).*

She was too shy to look him in the face.

He was shy in his high school days.

Reserved *[Adjective] (if you are reserved, you do not often talk about or show your feelings or thoughts).*

He is quite reserved when he is with strangers.

I found Tom very reserved.

Introverted *[Adjective] (someone who is a little quiet and shy and find it difficult to talk to other people).*

She is described as an introverted teenager, with a love of horses.

Her teachers perceived her as shy and introverted.

Quiet *[Adjective] (someone who does not usually talk much).*

He is by nature a very quiet person.

She was a very quiet child.

Timid *[Adjective] (shy and nervous).*

She is extremely nervous and timid.

Lucy is a rather timid child.

Confident *[Adjective] (if you are confident about something, you believe in your own abilities and do not feel nervous or frightened).*

She remains confident that she will get the promotion.

He seems very confident at work.

Ambitious *[Adjective] (having or showing a strong desire to be successful, rich, famous etc).*

He was an ambitious man with a strong personality.

She is brilliant, ruthless and ambitious.

Self-confident *[Adjective] (if you are self-confident, you trust in your abilities, qualities, and knowledge).*

Being tall can make him feel incredibly self-confident.

Eventually, she became more self-confident as a public speaker.

Self-assured *[Adjective] (having confidence and relaxation because you are sure of your abilities).*

He is experienced and self-assured.

She did her best to appear more self-assured than she felt.

Extroverted *[Adjective] (outgoing, lively and socially confident).*

Wilson was quite extroverted in his ability to speak to hundreds and thousands of people.

Mary is very friendly and extroverted so she should fit in quite easily.

Arrogant *[Adjective] (describing people who are too proud and look down on others (think they are better or more important than other people)).*

He thought he knew everything and was too arrogant to listen to his mentor's advice.

Tom is an arrogant boy.

He is not only arrogant but also selfish.

Angry *[Adjective] (very annoyed).*

At times, he gets very angry.

She was very angry with him.

Aggressive *[Adjective] (behaving in an angry or rude way).*

He is an aggressive person.

She sometimes is very aggressive and likes to start arguments.

Bad-tempered *[Adjective] (someone who easily becomes annoyed or angry).*

He was bad-tempered and graceless in defeat.

Why are you so bad-tempered today?

It is her illness that makes her bad-tempered.

Moody *[Adjective] (if you are moody, your mood changes suddenly and you become angry or unhappy easily for no particular reason).*

She doesn't know why she gets so moody sometimes.

He's a moody man. He can be happy one minute and angry the next.

Irritable *[Adjective] (having a tendency to become annoyed or impatient very easily).*

He was so irritable that everyone avoided him.

My baby gets irritable when woken up at night.

Don't take a call when you are irritable.

Charming *[Adjective] (very attractive and pleasant).*

You look very charming today.

He seems like a charming sort of guy.

Cheerful *[Adjective] (behaving in a happy, positive and friendly way).*

Tom and Mary both appear to be in a cheerful mood.

I was cheerful after I heard we won the game!

Vivacious *[Adjective] (lively, attractive, energetic and enthusiastic).*

She is a vivacious young lady.

He had three pretty, vivacious daughters.

Lively *[Adjective] (full of energy and enthusiasm; active and outgoing).*

My great grandma was a very lively person.

Though she is usually lively and energetic, Lucy seems calm today.

He played the guitar lively.

Helpful *[Adjective] (useful, or willing to help).*

I don't think that it is very helpful when first reading the book.

It's very helpful to bring a dictionary to my English class.

Sympathetic *[Adjective]* (showing or expressing sympathy (kind to someone and understand how they feel)).

She was very sympathetic when I was sick.

He was very sympathetic and kind.

Honest *[Adjective] (sincere; truthful).*

Just give me an honest answer.

Not everyone is honest.

Frank *[Adjective] (honest, sincere about the situation; telling the truth).*

He is frank with me about everything.

To be frank with you, I think he has little chance of passing the exam.

Reliable *[Adjective] (able to be trusted or believed).*

As far as I know, she is reliable.

The weather forecast is not necessarily reliable.

Although it is an old car, it's very reliable.

Genuine *[Adjective] (to be real and exactly; authentic).*

He hugged her with genuine feeling.

His sentiments and concerns are very genuine and his reasoning is very logical.

Sincere *[Adjective] (honest (not pretending or lying)).*

At first, he sounded very sincere.

I don't think that he is sincere.

She's a very sincere person when it comes to meeting people.

Gentle *[Adjective] (to be kind and calm).*

I think she is very kind and patient, and I love her very dearly.

He is a very kind man.

She's a very kind and thoughtful person.

Calm *[Adjective] (peaceful, quiet, and without worry).*

The most important thing to do now is for us to remain calm.

He tried to keep calm.

Loving *[Adjective] (feeling or showing love or great care towards someone).*

He's very loving and affectionate with his sister.

Old people need loving care and attention.

I have a very loving family.

Bright *[Adjective]* *(Intelligent, clever).*

He is bright, engaged, and interested in language and learning.

She is bright even if she does not study.

He is bright, intellectual and calm.

Talented *[Adjective]* *(to be very good at something).*

Tom is a very talented writer.

She's a very talented artist.

He's talented in mathematics.

Open-minded *[Adjective]* *(willing to consider new ideas).*

She was very open-minded.

My parents were very open-minded and didn't restrict our activities in any way.

Wise *[Adjective]* *(if you are wise, you are able to make good choices and decisions because you have a lot of understanding and experience).*

Old people are usually very wise.

She's a very wise mother.

Tom became wiser as he grew older.

Stupid *[Adjective]* *(not intelligent).*

He was stupid enough to believe what she said.

What a stupid man he is!

Immature *[Adjective]* *(not fully developed).*

He forgave his son's immature behaviour.

He's a nice little boy, a bit immature, but very intelligent.

Silly *[Adjective]* *(not intelligent).*

My friend was acting very silly, but it was fun.

He is very silly. He will believe anything.

Foolish *[Adjective]* *(silly, not intelligent).*

There are more foolish buyers than foolish sellers.

Tom felt foolish when he missed the point of the question.

Unrealistic *[Adjective]* *(impractical or impossible).*

Mary has unrealistic expectations.

The film was simplistic, silly, unrealistic and tedious.

Depressing *[Adjective]* *(something that makes someone feel very unhappy and disappointed).*

Black is depressing.

We found it a deeply depressing experience.

Unpleasant *[Adjective]* *(not enjoyable or discomfort).*

The weather is so unpleasant here.

I found his manner extremely unpleasant.

Frustrating *[Adjective]* *(making someone feel annoyed, impatient or less confident because they are prevented from achieving something).*

The current situation is very frustrating for us.

It was very frustrating to miss the train.

Disappointing *[Adjective]* *(failing to fulfill your hopes or expectations).*

The wine was excellent, but the food was disappointing.

His new movie is disappointing.

Embarrassing *[Adjective] (making someone feel nervous, ashamed, or stupid).*

It's really embarrassing trying to speak French because my accent is so poor.

It was a very embarrassing accident.

Embarrassed *[Adjective] (feeling ashamed or shy of something).*

He always mumbles when he's embarrassed.

She was embarrassed about how untidy the house was.

Incredulous *[Adjective] (unable to believe something).*

Many men are very incredulous.

He listened with an incredulous expression on his face.

Moved *[Adjective] (having a feeling of sadness or sympathy).*

What happened to that boy in the film was so awful. We were extremely moved.

I was very moved by his speech.

She was very moved and cried.

Pleased *[Adjective] (happy and satisfied with something).*

I was very pleased indeed to receive the invitation.

He is very pleased about getting his book published.

Delighted *[Adjective] (very happy).*

The crowd was delighted with the news.

I was delighted to meet you again.

He was delighted because he had found a new job.

Relaxing *[Adjective] (pleasant and making you feel relaxed).*

The holiday was relaxing.

She has a very relaxing way of speaking.

To sleep on top of a tree is very relaxing.

Comfortable *[Adjective] (feeling physically relaxed).*

Many women started to dress in comfortable clothes.

I lost my most comfortable shoes.

Peaceful *[Adjective] (calm and quiet; tranquil).*

Evening in the country is a very peaceful time.

Country life is very peaceful in comparison with city life.

Engrossing *[Adjective] (extremely interesting).*

He told us an engrossing story.

I am reading an engrossing book.

Exciting *[Adjective] (making you feel very happy or enthusiastic).*

I went to an exciting concert last night.

Some colours make us feel peaceful while others are exciting.

Energizing *[Adjective] (feeling full of energy or enthusiasm).*

Acupuncture has an energizing effect on mind and body.

Exercise is energizing.

Delightful *[Adjective] (very pleasant or enjoyable).*

It was delightful news for me.

Listening to my daughters' beautiful singing voices is always a delightful experience.

It's very delightful to see you!

Magnificent *[Adjective]* *(very impressive and beautiful)*.

The day was magnificent and the cool morning air as sharp as a knife.

The magnificent scene of the waterfall is pleasant.

PEOPLE OR THINGS DESCRIPTION/ PHYSICAL APPEARANCE

Appearance *[Noun] (the way that someone or something looks).*

You should not judge a person by his appearance alone.

Her appearance deceived him.

Figure *[Noun] (a person's body shape).*

His figure was tall, and as rigid and strong as cast-iron.

That dress shows off her figure to advantage.

Look = appearance *[Noun] (the way that a person looks).*

My brother has a very professional look when he is at work.

Her new haircut makes her look younger.

Identical to *[Adjective] (exactly the same; exactly alike).*

This picture is identical to the Picasso.

His car is identical to mine.

Pretty *[Adjective] (attractive).*

It's nice to have a pretty girl on each arm.

Because they are pretty, I love butterflies.

Attractive *[Adjective] (to be pleasant to look at).*

The thing he found most attractive about his girlfriend was her smile.

His wife is very attractive, and always gets lots of attention from the men at parties.

Courageous *[Adjective]* *(brave)*.

He was successful because he was courageous and stubborn.

People thought he was courageous, but he was quiet and cautious.

Generous *[Adjective]* *(to be very kind to other people (willing to give money, help, kindness, etc.))*

My uncle is generous with his money.

He has always been very generous toward the poor.

Grave *[Adjective]* *(looking very serious and worried)*.

He looked very grave as he entered the room.

The situation is becoming very grave.

Compact *[Adjective]* *(closely and neatly packed together)*.

These new compact digital cameras can fit in a shirt pocket.

The compact disc is a miracle of modern technology.

Sleek *[Adjective]* *(smooth, shiny)*.

She wore a sleek little black dress.

The actress looked stunning with her sleek hair and bold red lipstick.

Practical *[Adjective]* *(suitable for use in everyday life)*.

Varnished *[Verb]* *(to be painted with an oily liquid to make it shiny)*.

Don't sit on that chair. I've just varnished it.

The doors are then stained and varnished.

Airy *[Adjective]* *(describing a room with lots of light, fresh air and space)*.

This is a modern hotel with an airy, comfortable feel.

The large windows make the house light and airy.

Enormous *[Adjective] (very large in size or quantity)*.

He had enormous charm and a great sense of humour.

Their garden is very enormous.

Clingy *[Adjective] (wanting to be with someone all the time)*.

My dog is extremely clingy, refusing to leave my side no matter where I go.

Because she was so clingy, the girl never wanted to leave her boyfriend's side.

Dim *[Adjective] (not bright (insufficient amount of light))*.

Goldfish lose their color if they are kept in a dim light.

In the dim light, he couldn't see clearly and ran bump into a tree.

Murky *[Adjective] (dark, gloomy and dirty)*.

You will need a flashlight to explore the murky cave.

The light was too murky to continue playing.

Horrible *[Adjective] (very unpleasant)*.

Tom is in horrible shape.

It was really horrible and unbearable.

Disgusting *[Adjective] (extremely unpleasant)*.

The food in the restaurant was quite disgusting.

Her behavior was quite disgusting.

Awful *[Adjective] (very bad or unpleasant)*.

She looks awful when she cries.

He suffered awful injuries in the crash.

Unappealing *[Adjective] (unattractive or not interesting)*.

The town is scruffy and unappealing.

The food in the cafeteria was unappealing.

Impressive *[Adjective] (very good or awesome)*.

She has an impressive house.

I find her very impressive.

Thrilling *[Adjective] (extremely exciting)*.

The children were captivated by his thrilling story.

It was a thrilling experience.

The roller coaster ride was thrilling.

Untidy *[Adjective] (not arranged neatly and in order)*.

My son's terribly untidy; my daughter's no different.

She's got more untidy since she stopped going out to work.

Crumbling *[Adjective] (to break something into very small fragments or pieces)*.

It's an old, crumbling building.

The crumbling and old apartment building will be demolished soon.

LIKING AND DISLIKING

Be keen on *[Expression] (to be interested in; like).*

He is keen on playing football.

My sister is keen on Japanese food.

Be quite into something = be keen on something = be interested in something.

He's quite into fishing.

My father's quite into gardening.

I'm quite into swimming and diving.

Fond of *[Expression] (to love something or doing something very much).*

I am fond of fishing. He is fond of swimming.

My son is fond of playing games, but he understands his responsibility for studies.

To detest *[Verb] (to dislike someone or something very much).*

She thoroughly detests writing letters to him.

Lucy absolutely detests Tom.

Can't stand (someone or something) *[Verb] (to hate or dislike someone or something very much.)*

She can't stand to hear her parents arguing.

I can't stand traffic jam in rush hour.

Be passionate about *[Expression] (to have a strong desire to do something; really enjoy something).*

She is passionate about reading and writing novels.

He is passionate about teaching young children to read. Therefore, he has created his own tutoring business.

I am passionate about coffee. I drink it every day.

Have a passion for *[Expression]* *(a hobby or activity that someone loves to do very much)*.

I have a passion for fishing.

He has a passion for horse racing.

She has a passion for learning English.

IELTS WRITING VOCABULARY

Overall = general *[Adverb] (in all parts; taken as a whole).*

Overall, coffee production capacity tended to increase during this 10-year period.

Overall, the majority of people with university education were in younger age groups.

Fluctuations *[Noun] (changes in number or amount; a variation).*

Despite some minor fluctuations, this figure rose from about 15% in 2000 to 25% in 2010.

Significantly *[Adverb] (in a large or important way to be worthy of attention).*

Overall, the birth rate in China varied more significantly than in the US.

The percentage of couples who were married remained significantly higher than the other categories.

Steadily *[Adverb] (in an even and regular way).*

Although the consumption of coffee increased significantly to 120 tons in 2002, this fell steadily to just over 70 tons in 2005.

The percentage of commuters who used public transports increased steadily over the 10 years.

Consistently *[Adverb] (always in the same way).*

Overall, it is clear that the figures for all four indicators were consistently higher in Canada and Japan.

Sharply *[Adverb] (quickly, suddenly and by a large amount).*

Prices rose sharply for fresh fruits and vegetables, particularly after 1989.

The money spent on books rose sharply from $40 million in 2001 to $72 million in 2005.

The graph shows that the number of vehicles on the road is expected to continue to increase sharply.

In the following decade, the American birth rate fell sharply to below 5%.

By contrast/ In contrast *[Adverb] (these can be used to describe opposite/ different trend).*

In contrast, 10 years later, the birth rate in America decreased suddenly by over 15%, falling to approximately 3% in 2005.

By contrast, around 100 grams of beef was eaten, compared to about 60 grams of lamb in 2006.

Respectively = in turn.

The figures for lamb and beef were lower, at under 100 grams and exactly 80 grams respectively.

The spending figures for Italy and the UK were similar in 2005, at $60 million and $65 million, respectively.

The proportion = the percentage.

The line graph illustrates the proportion of people in four different age groups who went to the cinema in Great Britain from 1984 to 2000.

The chart illustrates the proportion of boys and girls who participated in various sports in New Zealand in 2002.

Figure *[Noun] (a number representing a particular amount).*

In the 1940s, the figure for the UK increased dramatically to exactly 20%, which was its highest point during the 50-year period.

The spending on chicken, beef, and lamb fell, while there was a steady increase in the figure for fish.

Slightly *[Adverb] (a little; not considerably).*

Approximately 10% of boys played badminton – the figure which was only slightly higher than girls for this sport.

At midday, the temperature increased almost 40 degrees before slightly decreasing in the afternoon.

Tended to increase *[Expression] (increased over a period of time).*

Overall, oil production capacity tended to increase during this 20-year period.

Although the rate of inflation fell in July and August, inflation tended to increase in the USA during 2015.

Reach a peak *[Expression] (the point at which something is at its highest quantity).*

Although the consumption of chicken reached a peak of about 300 grams in 1990, this fell steadily to just over 200 grams in 2005.

Having reached a peak of 47% in 1995, attendance among 16-23-year-olds was 75% in 2002.

To peak *[Verb] (reached its highest point).*

Although the oil amount fell in 2002 in the UAE, the figure peaked in 2005 in Iran with over 5 million barrels.

Expenditure = spending *[Noun] (the amount of money spent).*

The expenditure on beef, lamb, and fish decreased, while there was a fluctuating increase in the figure for chicken.

There was a steady increase in the spending on magazines in Sydney, and this finally reached a figure of $80 million in 2010.

Come a close second *[Expression] (be just behind another thing or person).*

Sorry, you came a close second.

A $60,000 scholarship must come a close second.

Double *[Adjective] (to twice the number or amount of something).*

The percentage figures for spending on transport and healthcare in Japan were double those for Malaysia.

It is also clear that the proportion of people who used a public library to obtain information in 2000 was double the figure for 1991.

Whereas = in contrast *[Conjunction] (used to contrast two facts).*

The expenditure figures for France and Australia were similar in 1990, at $65 million and $70 million, respectively, whereas the figure for Italy was much lower at just $40 million.

Overall, a higher percentage of students under 42 study to further their careers, whereas most over 60s study for interest.

In terms of *[Expression] (used to show which aspect of a subject you are discussing or writing about).*

Although the two countries' birth rate were similar in terms of a general fluctuation, the figure for China in most years was lower than that of the USA.

The line graph compares four areas in terms of the amount of oil consumed per day in a 22-year period starting in 2009.

Account for *[Expression] (to form a particular part or amount of something).*

The Japanese market accounted for 20% of our exports last year.

Grammar accounts for 25% of the marks in your writing test.

Fuel *[Noun] (a material that produces energy, power or heat when you burn it).*

Gasoline is used for fuel.

We're almost out of fuel.

The charts compare the units of electricity produced in New Zealand and Germany in 1980 and 2010 from 5 fuel sources.

While = whereas *[Conjunction] (used to indicate a contrast).*

By 2020, the number of barrels of oil consumed daily in the US is anticipated to fall to about 5 billion, while consumption is expected to decrease to 2 billion barrels in Western Europe.

While there were 70,000 prisoners in Australia in 1930, the number went down to about 40,000 in 1950.

Forecast *[Verb] (to predict or estimate (a future event or trend) based on the information that you have now).*

The overall sales for both companies are forecast to grow.

Until September, sales are predicted to remain unchanged at this level, after which they are estimated to rise steadily to roughly 1 million pairs in November.

Stable *[Adjective] (not likely to change, remaining constant; firmly fixed).*

While consumption fell in Western Europe/Japan by 2015, and remained stable in the US, there was an increase in oil consumption in China and the Middle East.

In spite of a slight increase in 2005, oil production in Iran remained relatively stable at more than 2 million barrels each day.

In preference to *[Expression] (instead of; rather than someone or something).*

Overall, cars are used in preference to other means of transport.

Because he had more experience, he was chosen for the job in preference to his brother.

Estimate *[Verb] (roughly/approximately calculate without knowing the number exactly).*

The forecast figure for UEA in 1995 was over 2 million barrels per day, compared with around 4 million barrels in the other two countries.

Police estimated that the number of people at the event was 15,000.

Anticipated *[Verb] (expected; estimated).*

It is estimated that sales of jeans will increase from 200,000 pairs in May to approximately 600,000 in December.

It is anticipated that the house will sell tomorrow.

Overtaking *[Verb] (become greater in number, or amount than something else).*

Nuclear power is overtaking oil as the main source of energy worldwide.

Over 35% of travellers used cars to go to work in this city in 2000, overtaking the figures for bus users (16%).

Steady *[Adjective] (not changing; firmly fixed).*

There was a steady rise in the spending on books in Italy, and this finally reached a figure of $65 million in 2000.

Although the percentage remained the lowest among the age groups, the proportion of the over 30s who went to the cinema witnessed a steady increase to 19% in 2005.

Vanished *[Verb] (disappeared suddenly).*

Overall, the number of houses rose significantly, whereas the lands for agricultural purposes vanished.

I looked everywhere for my cell phone, but I never found it - it seemed to have vanished!

Cut down *[Verb] (a decrease or reduction of the size, amount or number of something).*

His health will improve if he cuts down on cigarettes.

It is difficult to lose weight if you don't cut down on the amount you eat.

OTHER VOCABULARIES

LETTER A

Air *[Verb] (to air means to broadcast a program on TV or radio).*

My favorite TV show airs every weekend on a popular local channel at 6:00 p.m.

The Gadget Show airs on six channel each week.

At a crossroads *[Expression] (at an important point in someone's life when he/she has to make a very important decision).*

She was at a crossroads in her career.

I was at a crossroads with two choices - whether to join the army or to continue studying at university.

Aquatic animals *[Noun] (animals that live in water).*

Aquatic animals are negatively affected by overfishing, destructive fishing, and climate change.

Assign *[Verb] (to give a particular task to somebody to do).*

He does almost all the homework assigned every day.

Assigned homework helps keep students organized.

Alleyway *[Noun] (a narrow street or passageway).*

He brushed up against his boss in the alleyway.

We found a stray cat in the alleyway.

The police officer was very suspicious when he saw a suspicious man loitering in the alleyway.

As easy as it sounds = as easy as people think.

I assume it's not as easy as it sounds.

Pursuing our passions and dreams is never as easy as it sounds.

Acknowledge *[Verb] (accept, understand and admit)*.

He didn't acknowledge what she said.

He acknowledged his mistake.

I acknowledge it to be true.

As for *[Expression] (with regard to)*.

He prefers hiking and surfing. As for me, I would rather just stay at home and relax.

As for me, they are identical.

A bit *[Expression] (a little, a small amount)*.

His house is a bit of a mess.

It was a bit cold last night.

Advisable *[Adjective] (to be suggested or recommended)*.

Many doctors say that it is advisable to avoid coffee during pregnancy.

It is not advisable to drink too much.

Abundant *[Adjective] (existing in large quantities; more than enough)*.

The lake is abundant in fish.

Our country is abundant with natural resources.

Abandon *[Verb] (to leave something, or someone, usually forever; especially someone you are responsible for)*.

The house has looked abandoned since his family moved away 3 years ago.

The child was found abandoned but unharmed.

At heart *[Expression] (in someone's real nature).*

He's 80 years old, but he's still young at heart.

I still feel like a teenager at heart.

Alert *[Noun] (a warning to people to be prepared to deal with something dangerous that might happen soon).*

The tsunami alert was cancelled.

Be alert when you cross a busy street!

Awestruck *[Adjective] (feeling very surprised or impressed by something).*

He was awestruck when the announcer said his name during the awards presentation.

When Sarah's husband bought her a brand new house, she was awestruck.

Appetite *[Noun] (a natural desire for food).*

He suffered from a headache and a loss of appetite.

My brother does a lot of sports, so he has quite an appetite.

An inevitable consequence *[Noun] (certain to happen and unable to be avoided or prevented).*

It was an inevitable consequence of the decision.

Flooding, cyclones, and storms will be an inevitable consequence.

Appropriate *[Adjective] (suitable or proper for a particular purpose or situation).*

His speech on retirement was appropriate for his middle-aged audience.

For me, wearing jeans to the office is appropriate.

A concrete jungle *[Noun] (a way to describe a city that has many modern buildings and few green spaces, so it is unpleasant to live in).*

We survived in a concrete jungle.

This house was surrounded by fields; now it is in the middle of a concrete jungle.

A social butterfly *[Noun] (refers to an extrovert person who is social or friendly with everyone).*

He is a true social butterfly. He has friends on all of the sports teams.

Jane is definitely a social butterfly. She's got friends everywhere.

A high-flyer *[Noun] (someone who has the strong desire to be very successful).*

He's a self-made millionaire at the young age of 22! He's quite a high-flyer!

Her dad used to be a corporate high-flyer but after a stroke, he can't.

Adulation *[Noun] (excessive admiration or praise).*

The rock star enjoyed the adulation of his fans.

Her adulation to him was strong, stronger than she had planned for.

Avid *[Adjective] (very enthusiastic about something (often a hobby)).*

He was an avid fan of Chelsea football team.

She is an avid admirer of horror movies.

My father took an avid interest in politics.

A sense of accomplishment *[Expression] (a feeling of success in something or when you achieve something great).*

Having a baby gives them a sense of accomplishment.

Hiking up a mountain is hard work, but it provides a sense of accomplishment.

Attain *[Verb] (to succeed in achieving something that desires a lot of effort).*

He attained his goal.

After working hard for many years, she finally attained success as an author.

Aquatic life *[Noun]* *(the creatures and plants that live in the water for most or all of their lifetime).*

The chemicals which the factory put into the river killed all the aquatic life.

When you throw trash in the ocean, you endanger many species of aquatic life.

Altruism *[Noun]* *(the fact of willingness to do things that bring advantages and happiness to others more than your own).*

He was actuated almost entirely by altruism.

Social workers must have altruism.

An integral part of *[Expression]* *(play an essential part in something).*

It's a given that the Internet has become an integral part of our daily lives.

It goes without saying that grammar plays an integral part in learning English.

Having time to play with friends is an integral part of a happy childhood.

Adopt *[Verb]* *(to take up or start to use or follow a suggestion or a policy).*

Our boss has recently adopted a friendlier manner.

The government adopted a policy of increasing the tax on tobacco.

Her parents decided to adopt a child from Russia.

He was adopted as an infant.

Adoption *[Noun]* *(the act of starting to use something new).*

The widespread adoption of Western styles of clothes is a result of our modern way of life.

The adoption of a new policy on banning smoking in public places was supported by doctors.

Availability *[Noun]* *(the fact that something is suitable or ready for use).*

The overall widespread availability of inexpensive quality products.

Because they lived in a small town with limited resources, there was little availability of exotic fruits or vegetables.

More and more people are travelling by air owing to the availability of cheap flights.

Aspiration *[Noun]* *(a strong desire to do or achieve something).*

Peter has a strong aspiration to become rich.

From an early age, he has a strong aspiration to understand how a human mind works.

Autism *[Noun]* *(a mental problem in which a person finds it very difficult to communicate or form relationships with other people).*

Her son has autism. He is 10 and has very limited reading abilities.

Their child has autism and does not play with other children or speak to anyone.

Alarming *[Adjective]* *(causing people to feel danger, worried or frightened).*

The population of India is increasing at an alarming rate.

There is an alarming rise in the water level of the river.

(To) address *[Verb]* *(to deal with a problem).*

The government should address the environmental issues as soon as possible.

You should address the problem, and try to offer a solution to rectify the situation.

To act one's age *[Expression]* *(to behave in a mature manner).*

He doesn't look or act his age, she has no gray hairs, not even crows feet.

She looks and acts her age which is ten.

Attainment *[Noun]* *(the act of achieving or getting something)*.

She was offered the job because his educational attainments were very impressive.

His first full-time job is dependent upon his educational attainment and his father.

To allow = permit = let

They don't allow people to smoke in the hotel.

You can't enter the building without a permit.

She didn't intend to let him kiss her.

LETTER B

Be on one's way *[Expression] (be going, moving, travelling).*

When I met him in the street, I was on my way to my sister's house.

He is on her way to work/school.

Body language *[Noun] (the way that someone communicates nonverbally by moving his/her body).*

I could tell from her body language that she was very embarrassed.

He conveys information through his tone and body language.

Be there for *[Expression] (to be available to provide support for someone or to make him/her feel better).*

They haven't always been close, but he was there for her when she needed him.

Nobody was there for her when her boyfriend made her cry.

Bear in mind *[Expression] (remember/ keep in mind).*

Bear in mind that many poor people will need help.

Bear in mind what he said.

Be linked to *[Expression] (has a connection with).*

Agriculture is linked to economics and biology.

Blend into *[Expression] (to look very similar to the surrounding people or things, so that it is not easily noticeable).*

His black coat blended into the darkness.

The turtle's shell blended into the mud, making it almost invisible.

Barrier *[Noun] (a circumstance, problem or obstacle that prevents someone from doing something).*

Not having transportation was a barrier to the girl enrolling in college courses.

Age should not be a barrier to gaining access to university.

Based on *[Expression] (according to; to be the reason for something).*

We shouldn't judge people based on their appearance.

This story is based on a true story.

Her salary is based on commissions.

Breakthrough *[Noun] (an important achievement or development that comes after a lot of hard work).*

Scientists are claiming a major breakthrough in the fight against cancer.

A technical or scientific breakthrough is necessary.

To become obsolete *[Verb] (to be no longer used because something new has been invented).*

The machinery has become obsolete.

The invention of email has made hand-written letters obsolete.

To be out of one's depth *[Expression] (something that exceeds one's knowledge or ability because it is too difficult).*

The lesson was very hard, and he was completely out of his depth.

She felt totally out of her depth in her new job.

To become over-reliant on *[Expression] (to need something too much for your survival or success).*

We have become over-reliant on technology so much so that we cannot even imagine living without it.

Nowadays, people become over-reliant on Facebook to fulfill their social needs.

To be for the better *[Expression]* *(in a way that improves the situation).*

These changes seem to have been for the better.

My teachers' influences have been for the better, and I am wholeheartedly grateful for that.

LETTER C

Combination *[Noun] (a mixture of two or more things are combined to create something new).*

A clause is the combination of a subject and a verb.

The combination of science and art classes helps students learn in a creative way.

A clause is the combination of a subject and a verb.

A combination of several mistakes led to the accident.

Come across *[Verb] (to meet or find something or someone by chance).*

While she was cleaning out her desk, she came across some old pictures.

I never came across such a big snake in my life.

Catch one's eye *[Expression] (to attract someone's attention).*

A beautiful dress caught her eye while she was walking through the market.

A small shop selling lovely necklaces caught my eye while I was driving down the road.

Catch everything *[Verb] (to understand completely what someone said).*

I am able to catch everything you're saying.

The grammar checker won't catch everything.

It was so noisy that I was unable to catch everything.

(To) compensate *[Verb] (to pay money to someone in exchange for something that they have suffered).*

Since she paid over three hundred dollars for her dress, you cannot compensate her for its loss with a fifty dollar check.

The price of the car has been reduced to compensate for a defect.

The insurance company will compensate him for the loss.

Come up with *[Expression] (to suggest or think of an idea, solution or plan).*

He's come up with some amazing strategies to double his income.

She's come up with great techniques to help her through depression.

Crash *[Verb] (to hit something hard while moving and be damaged as a result).*

He crashed his car into a tree while driving home from a party.

The plane crashed soon after take off, but fortunately, no one was killed.

Compromise *[Noun] (an agreement or a settlement of a dispute).*

The two parties were unable to reach a compromise.

They compromised and made the sale for $500.

Complicated *[Adjective] (confusing, difficult to understand or explain).*

The machine is so complicated that no one is able to use it properly.

The process of fixing the car engine was complicated due to the lack of tools.

Chances are that *[Expression] (it's likely that).*

The chances are that she overslept this morning.

The chances are that he will be looking for a new job soon.

Current affairs *[Noun] (political and social events that are happening now).*

My father enjoyed reading newspaper about current affairs.

He is indeed interested in current affairs.

Charismatic *[Adjective] (having a personal quality to attract and impress other* *people).*

Martin Luther King was a very charismatic speaker.

They are very charismatic youngsters.

(To) crop up *[Verb] (to appear or happen unexpectedly).*

His name has cropped up at every selection meeting.

He has cropped up in connection with weapons, drugs, and sex trafficking.

To continue to thrive *[Expression] (to continue to grow, develop or be successful).*

They often worry if prisoners will continue to thrive on release.

Combat *[Verb] (to fight, struggle).*

The police are planning sterner measures to combat crime.

Exercise can help combat the effects of stress.

Complement *[Noun] (a thing that adds new qualities to something to make it better).*

The hat is a perfect complement to her outfit.

A fine whisky is a perfect complement to the dinner.

Capacity *[Noun] (the ability to understand or to do something).*

He was speaking in her capacity as a judge.

Her capacity for dissembling is limitless.

He has an enormous capacity for hard work.

Come in handy *[Expression] (to be useful or convenient).*

These boxes might come in handy one day.

This cardboard box just might come in handy one day. Don't throw it away.

Congenial *[Adjective] (friendly and pleasant).*

We found him charming and congenial.

The atmosphere in our colony is not congenial for serious studies.

Chant *[Noun]* *(words or phrases that a group of people shout or sing repeatedly).*

These catchy chants help students master their sight words.

The music was catchy chants.

We can't have a World Cup campaign without some catchy chants.

Come across *[Expression]* *(to meet or find someone/ something by chance).*

While she was cleaning out my desk, she came across this old picture.

I came across him on the bus.

Concerted *[Adjective]* *(done by several people or groups working together (in cooperation)).*

We need to make a concerted effort to finish the project on time.

She's making a concerted effort to improve her appearance.

He has begun to make a concerted effort to find a job.

Conventional *[Adjective]* *(traditional and ordinary; following what has been done in the past).*

He's very conventional in his views.

She prefers a more conventional style of dress.

Complementary *[Adjective]* *(two things which are different, but form a useful combination).*

His personality is complementary to hers.

Swimming and yoga are two complementary activities which help to reduce stress.

Convert *[Verb] (to change in form, character, or function).*

The church in our street has been converted into a restaurant.

Command *[Verb] (to deserve to obtain or achieve something).*

Skilled workers will be able to command high salaries and enjoy a decent standard of living.

With her skills and experience, she can command a high salary.

The best lawyers can expect to command a very high salary.

Confront *[Verb] (to deal with a problem or difficult situation or person).*

She has to confront her fears.

Never confront the teacher like you did.

Convince *[Verb] (to make someone believe that something is true).*

I was convinced by his explanation.

He wasn't able to convince her.

He was convinced of her innocence.

Countless *[Adjective] (too many to be counted).*

Countless stars lit up the night sky.

He is the idol of countless teenagers.

To code *[Verb] (to write code (numbers, words, and symbols) for a computer program).*

He got a job coding for Google.

Coding information into numbers and symbols requires advanced computer skills.

To cover a lot of ground *[Expression] (to deal with much information and many facts).*

We covered a lot of ground on our hike today.

We need to cover a lot of ground in French History before the exam date.

LETTER D

Deteriorate *[Verb] (to become worse in character, quality, value, etc).*

His health deteriorated rapidly, and he had to stop working in 2005.

Her health deteriorated quickly, and she soon died.

Draw attention *[Expression] (to make people notice something or someone).*

If we don't want to draw attention to the guards, please be quiet.

He dropped his wallet on purpose to draw her attention.

Do not take someone or something lightly = take someone or something seriously *[Expression] (regard something or someone as vital and worthy of attention).*

His parents threatened to punish him, but he didn't take them seriously.

Career choices can be incredibly difficult to make, and I do not take them lightly as a recruiter.

Getting married and choosing to have kids are two major decisions in your life, do not take them lightly.

Deplete *[Verb] (to reduce something in size or amount (by a large amount)).*

This expense has depleted our funds.

Our stock of food is greatly depleted.

Drawbacks *[Noun] (a disadvantage or problem).*

The drawbacks of the new hospital are the location and the building costs.

There are certain drawbacks to life outside the city.

Date *[Noun] (a romantic meeting with a male or female).*

They decided to remain just good friends although they had several dates.

Do (or try) one's best *[Expression]* *(to try very hard/ do as much as possible to achieve something).*

He has tried his best to repair the TV but still is not working.

I tried my best to get here on time.

Disregard *[Verb]* *(to pay no attention to someone or something).*

She disregarded him, and her words insulted him.

He completely disregarded me and threatened me.

Despite the fact that *[Expression]* *(even though).*

Despite the fact that Tom studied very hard, he didn't pass the exam.

She is very slim despite the fact that she eats a lot.

Dusk *[Noun]* *(partial darkness; the time when the sun has gone down).*

The sky at dusk is red.

The street lights come on at dusk and go off at dawn.

Depend on *[Verb]* *(to rely on someone for help).*

She depends on her parents for her university fees.

He depends on his father for everything.

Distract *[Verb]* *(to prevent someone from concentrating on something).*

I do not want to distract her mind from her lessons.

The music distracted him from his work.

Draw lots *[Verb]* *(to decide who will do something by picking cards, tickets or numbers from a container by chance).*

We had to draw lots to decide who would go.

They drew lots to decide who should go first.

Desirable *[Adjective] (that you would like to have or do; worth having or doing because it is useful, necessary).*

Because the concert tickets were desirable, they sold out quickly.

Because he had a pleasant demeanor, he was a desirable friend.

The house has many desirable features, and lots of people would love to buy it.

Degradation *[Noun] (the process of something becoming worse or damaged).*

Whatever the degradation, the human spirit can be indestructible.

He was forced to suffer the degradations of poverty and abuse.

Some feel that violence on television has caused a degradation of society.

Disorder *[Noun] (a problem or illness that causes someone's mind or body to stop functioning properly).*

She suffers from a rare disorder of the liver, so many doctors had not seen a case like this before.

Respiratory disorders are affected by air pollution in cities.

Dependent *[Adjective] (be relying on someone or something in order to survive or to be successful).*

People cannot solely be dependent on luck to become successful.

Developing countries nowadays are heavily dependent on natural resources to drive their economy, especially in transportation and energy fields.

Disincentive *[Noun] (something that makes someone less willing to do something (discourage people from doing something)).*

A sudden fall in profits provided a further disincentive to new investors.

High taxes are a disincentive to business.

Distinctive *[Adjective] (having a quality that makes something different and easily noticed from others).*

My teacher has a distinctive approach to teaching English. Unlike the other teachers, he does not teach any grammar.

Each of the performers is distinctive because of his or her unique appearance or affectation.

Deterrent: *[Noun] (a thing that discourages someone from doing something (makes somebody less likely to do something).*

Long prison sentences can be a very effective deterrent for offenders.

Cameras are a major deterrent to crime.

Dependence on *[Noun] (the state of needing something or someone all the time in order to survive or be successful).*

A young baby has a great dependence on her parents.

Gradually his dependence on alcohol became obvious to everyone.

Due to *[Expression] (because of; owing to; as a result of).*

The war had an adverse impact on the environment, due to all the chemicals that were sprayed.

The cancelation was due to rain.

Durable *[Adjective] (likely to last for a long time without becoming damaged).*

The couple was searching for a durable car that would last years.

These are the only tools that are durable enough for the job.

Discourage *[Verb] (make somebody feel less confident, enthusiastic or less willing to do something).*

He is never discouraged by difficulties.

She discouraged me from undertaking the work.

The bad weather discouraged people from attending the event.

Dispose of *[Verb] (to throw away or get rid of something that you no longer want or need)*.

Dispose of these old newspapers.

I dispose of my trash in the garbage can.

Discerning *[Adjective] (able to show good or outstanding judgment and understanding about the quality of something)*.

She had a discerning eye for color.

In order to be at the top of your field as a mechanic, you must be very discerning and not miss any details.

Decent *[Adjective] (of a good or acceptable standard or quality)*.

With this much money, I could buy a very decent used car.

Tom hasn't eaten a decent meal in a long time.

It's hard to find a decent restaurant in this town;

Deterioration *[Noun] (the process of becoming progressively worse)*.

As she watched the deterioration of her parents' marriage, she prayed they would divorce soon.

There has been a serious deterioration of his mental condition.

There is a deterioration in the relations between the two countries.

Decorative *[Adjective] (intended to make something or someone look more attractive or pretty)*.

Many people in the art gallery have been attracted by decorative paintings.

Decorative sculptures are often a part of Japanese-style landscapes.

Disappointment *[Noun] (the feeling of frustration, sadness or displeasure)*.

The saddened father's face was filled with disappointment when he found out his daughter had lied to him.

After Sarah didn't make the cheerleading team, she was filled with a feeling of disappointment.

LETTER E

To enjoy something to the fullest *[Expression] (to enjoy something as much as possible).*

My goal is to enjoy life to the fullest.

College is the time to enjoy yourself to the fullest!

End up *[Expression] (to find oneself in a situation or place that was not planned or expected to be in).*

After he killed his wife, he ended up in jail.

If we'd looked where we were going, we wouldn't have ended up in such a mess.

If he carries on shoplifting, he'll end up in jail.

Evocative *[Adjective] (making you remember or imagine something pleasant).*

His new book is wonderfully evocative of village life.

The taste of the cakes was evocative of my childhood.

Extravagant *[Adjective] (costing too much money than you can afford or is necessary).*

The diamond necklace was far too extravagant for a simple dinner party.

The house is well out of my price range because it is so extravagant.

Extraction *[Noun] (the act or process of removing something, especially using effort or force).*

The extraction of salt from the sea has been practised for many centuries.

The extraction of fossil fuels, such as oil, gas, and coal to satisfy increasing energy demands has serious environmental impacts.

Emulate *[Verb] (try to imitate with effort to equal or surpass someone who you admire).*

The boy would emulate his father's morning routine, from reading the newspaper to sipping coffee.

She hopes to emulate her sister's success as a dancer.

Exclude *[Verb] (to prevent someone or something from taking part an activity or entering a place).*

Tom is excluded from the list of people present at the party.

For many years, women were excluded from sports such as football and basketball.

Enlighten *[Verb] (provide someone with information so that they understand a subject or situation better).*

He enlightened me on this subject.

He holds a very enlightened attitude toward working women.

Enlightening *[Adjective] (providing you more information, insight, and understanding of something).*

That was a very enlightening programme.

It was a very enlightening interview.

Elaborate on *[Verb] (explain about).*

Could you elaborate more on this idea?

Ethnic minority *[Noun] (a group of people living in a country or area in which most people have a different culture and different traditions.)*

Discrimination against ethnic minorities is prohibited by law in most countries.

The populations of ethnic minorities have increased significantly over the period of 10 years.

(To) extend *[Verb] (to make something longer, wider or larger).*

The woods extend for miles to the west.

The table measures seven feet long when it is fully extended.

To empower women *[Verb] (to give women the freedom to do something).*

Sport has huge potential to empower women and girls.

Gender equality will only be reached if we are able to empower women.

LETTER F

For good *[Expression]* *(forever; permanently).*

He's gone for good.

He has left London for good.

Forget all about *[Expression]* *(to forget completely).*

To tell the truth, I forgot all about your questions.

I forgot all about paying the bill.

She forgot all about her assignment.

From scratch *[Expression]* *(to start from the very beginning).*

He built his business from scratch.

She came from a very poor family, she started her own career from scratch.

Fully intend to *[Expression]* *(to have a definite objective or plan to do something).*

She had fully intended to tell him exactly what had happened.

He fully intended to pay for the damage.

Fed up *[Adjective]* *(bored, unhappy or disappointed, especially with a situation that has continued for a long time).*

They are fed up with the noise and bustle of the big city.

Tom is fed up with his job.

Faculty *[Noun]* *(a department within a university or college).*

My favorite teacher of the French faculty is Mr. John. He is very nice and friendly with students.

My favorite member of the faculty here at school is Miss. White, because she teaches my favorite class.

Fortunately *[Adverb] (luckily; in a lucky manner).*

Fortunately, the bus was late so he did not miss it.

Fortunately, nobody was at home when the bomb exploded.

Foremost *[Adverb] (the most important (first in place, order)).*

This question has been foremost in my mind recently.

A parent should be foremost a listener.

To fall by the wayside *[Expression] (if something falls by the wayside, it fails to continue/ people stop doing it).*

Many clubs fall by the wayside for financial reasons.

Luxury items fall by the wayside during a recession.

Flawless *[Adjective] (perfect, without defects or faults).*

All the stones are flawless and of the finest quality.

He can't help noticing her flawless beauty.

Force *[Verb] (to use physical strength, or power to make somebody do something that they do not want to do).*

He was forced to take the exam again, because he failed last month.

After seeing the evidence, he was forced to admit his error.

Far and wide *[Expression] (over a large area).*

He ranges far and wide in search of inspiration for his paintings.

People came from far and wide to see the concert.

Fierce competition *[Noun] (strong competition/ tough competition.)*

Graduates face fierce competition in getting jobs.

Small grocery stores face very fierce competition from the large supermarket chains.

Fake *[Adjective]* *(not genuine; counterfeit (in order to trick people))*.

The child was wearing fake fangs to go with his vampire costume.

He bought a fake diamond ring for his girlfriend at the fair for a joke.

Fool around *[Verb]* *(to behave in a silly way for fun)*.

Don't fool around with matches.

You shouldn't fool around with dangerous chemicals.

To fuel *[Verb]* *(to make something increase or stronger)*.

Lower interest rates have fuelled a housing boom in the country.

Salary increases and high food prices fuelled inflation last year.

LETTER G

Go out of one's way (to do something) *[Expression]* *(to make a special effort to do something)*.

Sarah really went out of her way to make me feel welcome.

Tom went out of his way to be friendly/kind.

Glossy: *[Adjective]* *(smooth and shiny, so as to look real and attractive)*.

She has glossy black hair.

My cat has glossy black fur.

We commit to providing customers with outstanding service.

Get through *[Expression]* *(to successfully deal with a problem or overcome a difficulty)*.

There are too many items on the agenda for the meeting to get through.

It took me about an hour to get through customs at the airport when I got home from my holidays.

Gratitude *[Noun]* *(the feeling of being thankful or grateful)*.

She felt gratitude for the gifts that poured down upon her.

His heart was filled with gratitude.

Generally speaking *[Expression]* *(used to describe a general feeling or opinion about something)*.

Generally speaking, boys like active sports more than girls do.

Generally speaking, college students have more free time than high school students.

Get to grips with *[Expression]* *(to make an effort to handle or deal with something difficult).*

He should get to grips with his fear of public speaking.

(To) get access to *[Expression]* *(to get the right to use something or enter a place).*

We can't get access to the building without the permission of the owner.

How did the spy get access to the secret information?

Go viral *[Expression]* *(spread quickly and widely through the Internet).*

His song went viral on social media.

Her video went viral on YouTube.

To gain access to the internet/to access the internet *[Expression]* *(to have a chance to use the internet).*

I need a computer which can gain access to the internet.

Students are able to access the Internet anywhere, including in classrooms.

Go to great lengths to do something *[Expression]* *(put a great deal of effort to accomplish something).*

He went to great lengths to prove his point.

She went to great lengths to assist her mate.

Grossly *[Adverb]* *(extremely; excessively – used to describe something unpleasant or untrue).*

Medical records were found to be grossly inadequate.

After many years of eating too much, she is grossly overweight.

Genuine leather *[Noun]* *(real leather).*

That football is made of genuine leather.

In fact, genuine leather does not mean high-quality leather.

LETTER H

High degree of *[Noun] (high level of).*

He was suffering a high degree of stress.

Highly credible *[Adjective] (very trustful).*

The story he told me was highly credible.

Her testimony was highly credible.

To hinder *[Verb] (to make it difficult for somebody to do something or for something to happen).*

The power outage hindered his ability to get his research done.

The storm hindered our progress.

Humane *[Adjective] (showing compassion, kindness, and sympathy towards others).*

It is not humane to kill animals for food.

He became great because of his humane qualities.

Haunt *[Noun] (a place that a specified person or group of people frequently visit or where they spend a lot of time).*

The area was a popular tourist haunt.

The terrace, which overlooks the park, was a favourite haunt of lovers.

To hide one's light under a bushel *[Expression] (if you hide your light under a bushel, you keep your talents or accomplishments hidden from other people).*

He has some good ideas, but he doesn't speak very often. He hides his light under a bushel.

Mary is an excellent singer but she tends to hide her light under a bushel and won't sing in public.

Have yet to *[Expression] (if you have yet to do something, you have not done or completed it).*

I have yet to read that book.

He has yet to make the decision.

She has yet to appear at the party.

Host country *[Noun] (a country hosting an event).*

Spain is the host country for the Olympics in 1992.

Chile is the host country for this year's conference.

Huge number of *[Expression] (an extremely large amount of something).*

There are a huge number of exceptions to these rules.

They have a huge number of fans who are inspired by their actions.

Hard-wearing *[Adjective] (that lasts a long time and remains in a good condition even if it is used a lot).*

Western clothes are usually hard-wearing, although this depends on the quality and price.

I use these shoes for work every day. They are very hard-wearing.

Home life *[Noun] (your life at home; private life).*

Her home life is affecting her work.

Balancing work and home life is an important part of our success.

To have social skills *[Verb] (to have the personal skills that you use to successfully communicate and interact with each other).*

Having great social skills help you get an ideal job easily and progress rapidly in your career.

To have a head for sth *[Expression] (to have a natural ability to do or understand something well).*

She should go in for accounting because she has a good head for figures.

He has a good head for mathematics.

To have a laid-back attitude *[Expression] (relaxed, not worrying about anything).*

She had a laid-back attitude about her exams.

He always had a laid-back attitude toward life.

LETTER I

Indulge *[Verb] (to allow someone to enjoy something that they want or desire).*

Parents should not allow their children to indulge themselves playing computer.

He indulges himself with many luxuries.

Illustrate one's point *[Expression] (prove one's point, or use as an example).*

My father always used examples from his own life experience to illustrate his point.

The priest cited a passage from the Bible to illustrate his point.

Individuality *[Noun] (uniqueness of character of a particular person).*

Many teenagers try to express their individuality by dressing in a certain way.

She dyes her hair, pierces her body, and dresses uniquely to express her individuality.

Irrespective of *[Expression] (regardless of, no matter what).*

Everyone must receive the vaccination, irrespective of age or sex.

She did it irrespective of all the advice she was given.

(To) integrate *[Verb] (to join a group).*

He found it difficult to integrate into Indian culture.

They have not made any effort to integrate into the local community.

It's not an indication of *[Expression] (it doesn't mean (that)).*

It's not an indication of serious mental illness.

It's not an indication of failure.

Inevitably *[Adverb] (will happen no matter what/ unavoidably).*

Excessive drug use will inevitably lead to an addiction.

He will inevitably hurt himself because he takes too many risks.

In jeopardy *[Expression] (in danger).*

If she does not take your medicine, she will put her health in jeopardy.

Their children are in jeopardy.

Inappropriate *[Adjective] (not suitable or proper for a particular purpose or situation).*

Some people felt that his behavior was inappropriate.

The movie's subject matter is inappropriate for small children.

Impact *[Noun] (a strong effect or influence on someone or something).*

Homelessness can often have a negative impact on local communities.

The overuse of social media and technology has a negative impact on young generation.

Irreplaceable *[Adjective] (impossible to be replaced).*

Although Tom loved riding the train, he knew that the time with his grandfather was irreplaceable.

The antique door was irreplaceable.

Initial *[Adjective] (happening at the beginning).*

After the initial excitement, she quickly became bored.

Initial reports say that seven people have died, though this has not yet been confirmed.

It's no wonder *[Expression] (it is not surprising).*

It's no wonder that the baby is crying.

It's no wonder he lost the game.

Intrigue *[Verb] (to make somebody very curious or interested about something).*

The plan intrigues me, but I wonder if it will work.

He's been intrigued by her since they met.

Intrigued by the new scents, she began opening bottles to smell them.

In bloom *[Expression] (the state of having flowers opening).*

All the beautiful flowers are in bloom now.

The roses are in full bloom.

Our apple tree is blooming.

In the vicinity of *[Expression] (near; close to (a place)).*

The stolen car was found in the vicinity of the mall.

We live in the vicinity of the school.

Immeasurable *[Adjective] (too large, extensive or great to be measured).*

His films had an immeasurable effect on a generation of Japanese.

The typhoon caused immeasurable damage.

Invariably *[Adverb] (always).*

He was invariably late for work every day.

He invariably had his coffee by 6 o'clock.

My mom invariably gets up early, even on the weekends.

Implement *[Verb] (to put something into effect).*

A new work programme for young people will be implemented by the government.

Some measures can be implemented to encourage people to take up walking as part of their daily routine.

Inequalities *[Noun] (the quality of being unequal or uneven).*

There are economic inequalities between different regions of the country.

Increasing levels of poverty and rising wealth inequalities impact on the economic growth of a country and the security of its citizens.

Initiative *[Noun] (a new plan or process to deal with something, such as a problem).*

The government has adopted several initiatives to deal with unemployment.

He takes the initiative in helping his mother do the housework.

Immerse *[Verb] (to become completely involved in something).*

He got some books out of the library and immersed himself in Chinese history and culture.

She had immersed herself in writing short stories.

In advance *[Expression] (before a certain time; before you do something else).*

Can you pay me in advance?

Thank you in advance for your cooperation.

Intimidating *[Adjective] (making you feel nervous, less confident, or frightened).*

It's a bit intimidating.

He finds it very intimidating to speak in front of a large number of people.

LETTER K

Known reasons *[Noun] (reasons that people already know about).*

There is no known reason for the accident.

There are many known reasons for the lack of interest in electoral politics, like the fact that only rich people can run for president.

LETTER L

Leap *[Verb]* *(to make a quick or sudden movement).*

When the alarm went off, she leapt out of bed.

A mouse leapt out of the cereal box and frightened everyone.

He leapt out of his car and ran towards the house.

To lose track of something *[Expression]* *(to lose or lose sight of something).*

I've lost track of that new coat he gave me.

Tom probably lost track of time and is in a dead zone.

Lose one's patience *[Expression]* *(if someone loses his/her patience, he/she is unable to keep his/her temper, and become suddenly angry).*

He lost his patience and decided to attack the young man.

The woman lost her patience and assaulted the boy.

Lose the chance *[Expression]* *(lose the opportunity).*

I lost the chance to spend a year abroad.

Lose faith *[Verb]* *(Don't trust anymore).*

Don't lose faith in yourself.

We do not lose faith in God.

Loyal *[Adjective]* *(to be faithful and devoted to someone or something).*

He is very loyal to his friends.

She is a very loyal customer.

To lie in the heart of sth *[Expression]* *(to be in the center of somewhere).*

Kazakhstan lies in the heart of a Central Asian region.

The building lies in the heart of the city.

Long-term *[Adjective]* *(taking place a long period of time).*

The indiscriminate use of fertilizers can cause long-term problems.

We want long-term solutions.

(To) lag behind *[Verb]* *(to move or develop more slowly than someone or something else).*

We still lag far behind many of our competitors in using modern technology.

The salaries of teachers continue to lag far behind other college-educated professionals.

To launch a product *[Expression]* *(to introduce a new product).*

We're going to launch a new product, but we're not sure how to get started.

You don't need a huge PR machine to successfully launch a new product.

To long for *[Verb]* *(to want something very much/ to desire for something).*

The long summer holiday is longed for by most children.

He longed for a cold drink in the hot weather.

Limbs *[Noun]* *(arms and legs of a person or animal).*

After the car accident, he lost the use of his limbs; now, however, he can walk and use his hands normally.

Lottery *[Noun]* *(a type of gambling game in which people buy numbered tickets to win a prize).*

As the way of my thinking, any person who wins a lottery is absolutely lucky.

My brother always goes to the shop every week to buy lottery tickets, but he never wins.

Low priority *[Noun] (something that you think is not urgent and less important than other things).*

He will get to the low priority tasks later.

Government spending on the arts is a low priority during times of economic crisis.

Let one's hair down *[Expression] (to enjoy yourself in a relaxed manner).*

When she took off her glasses and let her hair down, she was incredibly beautiful.

Regardless of what her parents said, she wanted to let her hair down that night.

LETTER M

Mainly *[Adverb] (more than anything else).*

His essay was mainly about the importance of zoos, although it also contained a discussion of wild animals.

The group is made up of mainly male students.

Muscular development *[Noun] (the process of making muscles become stronger).*

He goes to the gym every day to increase his muscular development and flexibility

To the full *[Adverb] (to the greatest possible degree).*

Our aim is to enjoy life to the full.

Match *[Verb] (to fit, be equal, or similar (colour, size or style)).*

The words on his T-shirt doesn't match with him.

This carpet does not match the curtain.

Move out of *[Expression] (to leave the place where you are living now (house, apartment, etc.)).*

Jack moved out of his apartment in London last month.

She finally moved out of her parents' house.

Means a lot to someone *[Expression] (something that is meaningful or important to someone).*

The gift means a lot to me.

It means a lot to him to know that you believe him.

My home life means a lot to me.

Models *[Noun] (people whose job it is to wear and show new styles of clothes).*

Do women really want to look like fashion models?

I think fashion models today are too thin.

Makes it possible *[Expression] (allows/enables).*

The scholarship made it possible for her to continue her education.

Medical advances have made it possible to keep more patients alive.

Majority *[Noun] (the greater number or part of something).*

A majority of students dislike history.

The majority of the employees have college degrees.

Mingle *[Verb] (to mix or combine something with something else).*

She felt a kind of happiness mingled with regret.

Her essence is green mingled with blue.

(To) memorize *[Verb] (to learn by heart).*

I don't try to memorize speeches word for word.

He can memorize facts very quickly.

To make the grade *[Expression] (to successfully reach a particular standard).*

As a child, she wanted to be a singer but failed to make the grade.

Not a lot of athletes make the grade in professional sports.

Maintenance *[Noun] (the process of preserving something).*

People from rich families can afford to pay tuition fees and for their own maintenance during their studies.

His part-time job paid for his maintenance while he was studying.

Mindless *[Adjective] (not requiring much mental effort (thought or intelligence)).*

Doing mindless work all day is going to drive me crazy.

At work, we have to do mindless and repetitive tasks.

Mass *[Noun] (a large number or amount of something).*

A mass of students took part in the demonstration.

The forest is a mass of colour in autumn.

Mass-produced *[Adjective] (produced in large quantities, usually by machinery).*

Stay away from mass-produced items, and look for the more original high-quality hand-crafted items.

They seem to be mass produced by machines.

Mogul *[Noun] (a very rich, important and powerful person).*

As a real estate mogul, Trump has made billions of dollars.

He is a famous movie mogul, making his fortune in Hollywood.

Minor *[Adjective] (small or insignificant).*

He had a minor accident this morning.

She had a minor operation last week.

LETTER N

Nominate *[Verb] (to formally suggest or propose someone as a candidate for an important role, prize/award, position, etc).*

He was nominated as the country's vice-president.

He was nominated to speak on our behalf.

Novelist *[Noun] (someone who writes novels).*

Besides being a lawyer, he is a very famous novelist.

As a novelist, he is famous for his difficulty.

The needy *[Noun] (poor people).*

We should help the poor and the needy.

The city supplied the needy with food and clothes.

Nerve-racking *[Adjective] (making someone feel very nervous and worried).*

His wedding was the most nerve-racking thing he's ever experienced.

It's nerve-racking watching him climb.

Night lamp = night light *[Noun] (a lamp kept burning during the night, especially in a bedroom).*

The modern style table with the night lamp in the bedroom.

The naked eye *[Noun] (the normal power of your eye without the help of any special device for making images larger (a telescope, microscope, or other devices.)*

You can see it with the naked eye.

Bacteria are invisible to the naked eye.

Needy *[Adjective]* *(lacking money, food, clothes; very poor).*

They awarded scholarships to needy students.

He treats needy and poor with sympathy.

Notable drawbacks *[Noun]* *(disadvantages which are important to note).*

But just like with Facebook, there are some notable drawbacks to using Twitter.

Despite its success, this approach has notable drawbacks.

Negative factor *[Noun]* *(factor that is not good and negatively affects something else).*

A negative factor is that getting pregnant after 35 years of age oftentimes carries more potential health risks.

The one negative factor about this job is that I have to get up so early.

Novelty *[Noun]* *(the quality of being new, different, unique or unusual).*

There's a certain novelty value in this approach.

We like novelty in our day to day life.

Neglected *[Verb]* *(to pay no attention to someone or something).*

The reason he failed was because he neglected his work.

When an opportunity is neglected, it never comes back to you.

She neglected to do her homework, so my teacher scolded her.

LETTER O

Overlook *[Verb] (to have a view of/from).*

We had a party in an Italian restaurant overlooking a river.

Open to *[Adjective] (be willing to receive or welcome).*

The club is open to people of all ages.

I'm open to new opportunities.

On purpose *[Expression] (intentionally; deliberately).*

He came here on purpose to see me.

He didn't do it on purpose - it was an accident.

Obstacle *[Noun] (something that makes it difficult for you to move forward or achieve something else).*

There is no obstacle for any journalist to express whatever he thinks.

A tree fell across the road and became an obstacle for cars and trucks.

Out of the question *[Expression] (impossible).*

I'm afraid a promotion is out of the question now.

It is out of the question to digest his theory.

Outdated *[Adjective] (no longer useful, because it is old-fashioned (out of date)).*

His writing style is now boring and outdated.

We must not use outdated security system.

Outweighed *[Verb] (greater or more significant than something).*

The dangers of surfing are outweighed by the excitement of this sport.

He outweighs me by 8 kg.

Opt for *[Verb] (to make a choice from a range of options).*

Tom opted for early retirement.

After she graduated, she opted for a career in music.

To be overprotective *[Adjective] (tending to protect someone, especially a child, excessively).*

My wife is overprotective of everyone.

Their mother suffocated them with overprotective love.

Overload *[Noun] (an excessive amount; to give someone too much work to do).*

The donkey was so overloaded, it could hardly climb the hill.

He has overloaded his schedule with work, study, and family responsibilities.

LETTER P

Potentially *[Adverb] (be likely to develop or happen in the future).*

This drug is potentially harmful to human health.

Smoking will not kill him immediately, but it is potentially harmful to his health.

Portable device *[Noun] (any device that can easily be held, carried or moved).*

Portable devices such as MP3 players, laptops, cell phones are becoming increasingly popular.

Billions of portable devices are sold around the world.

Perspective *[Noun] (a way of thinking about something).*

When she spoke, her perspective surprised him.

His perspective on things is different.

Pestering *[Verb] (annoying someone by asking them for something repeatedly).*

A teenage boy was pestering his mother for money.

Lucy was pestering her mother for a story every morning after breakfast.

Politely decline *[Verb] (to politely refuse).*

His offer was politely declined.

I offered to bear all the expenses but they politely declined.

Practical *[Adjective] (suitable for use in everyday life).*

His idea is practical.

Tom gave Mary some practical advice.

Provide *[Verb] (to give something to someone; to supply).*

The company provides health care and life insurance benefits for all of its employees.

He always provides me with good input.

Purpose *[Noun] (an aim, an objective or goal).*

This room is used for various purposes.

The site is used for education purposes.

Precious *[Adjective] (very valuable or important and not to be treated carelessly).*

Time is a precious thing, so we should make the best use of it.

Clean water is a precious commodity in the world.

Primarily *[Adverb] (mainly).*

This dictionary is primarily intended for high school students.

Hydropower is used primarily to generate electricity.

Poverty-stricken *[Adjective] (extremely poor, almost without any money).*

They are poverty-stricken, and easily fall victim to fever.

We wandered through a poverty-stricken village in the countryside.

Priority *[Noun] (something that is very important and must be done first).*

Education cannot afford to be a priority, but it should be.

The government should give top priority to rebuilding the inner cities.

To put up with *[Expression] (to accept or tolerate something that is annoying or unpleasant).*

They have to put up with a lot of noise when their children are at home.

He has to put up with a lot of stress, but he still enjoys spending time with his grandmother.

Persistence *[Noun] (the act of continuing to do something despite difficulties).*

Her persistence in asking for a raise was finally rewarded.

His persistence finally won him the prize.

Prevalent *[Adjective] (widespread in a particular place).*

These diseases are more prevalent among young children.

Drugs, and under-age drinking are prevalent among teenagers.

Patronage *[Noun] (the support and money given to a person by an individual or organization).*

The president manages patronage for the party.

Provide a link to our roots *[Expression] (to connect with previous generations).*

They provide a link to our roots, and they are part of our shared heritage.

Preparation *[Noun] (something done to get ready for an event or make something ready).*

Cutting vegetables in preparation for making soup.

I am making plans in preparation for my son's wedding.

To push forward *[Expression] (to advance something; to continue doing something or making progress in something despite difficulties or opposition).*

Our goals are to push forward, not pull back.

We must push forward with our plans.

The soldiers pushed forward to attack the enemy.

(To) possess *[Verb] (to have or own something).*

The old man possesses great wealth.

My uncle possessed a large house and two cars.

To pull something off *[Expression] (to succeed in doing or achieving something difficult).*

Peter pulled off a surprise victory in the semi-final.

We pulled off the deal.

Purely *[Adverb] (completely; entirely).*

From a purely practical point of view, the house is too small.

They have been given college scholarships purely on athletic ability.

Pitfalls *[Noun] (a hidden or unsuspected danger or difficulty, which it is not easy or possible to see at first).*

The mistakes could be avoided if a learner knows the pitfalls.

His advice helped me avoid some of the common pitfalls.

Privilege *[Noun] (a special right, or advantage granted to someone to have the chance to do something).*

I am giving my son the privilege of being able to stay out till midnight on Saturday nights.

Put off *[Verb] (to delay doing something).*

Never put off until tomorrow what you can do today.

Don't put off your homework to the last minute.

We heard that the weather was bad, so we decided to put off our trip.

Popularize *[Verb] (to make something become popular so that a lot of people know about it).*

Holidays in Thailand have been popularized through advertising on TV.

The book presents a popularized version of American history.

Pick something up *[Verb]* *(to lift something up and take it away)*.

Don't pick up the cat.

I want to stop by the bakery to pick up some fresh bread.

To prey on *[Verb]* *(to hurt or deceive someone, especially who is weaker than you)*.

Foxes prey on rabbits.

Criminals sometimes use social networks to prey on young people and involve them in the sex trade.

Permanently *[Adverb]* *(lasting forever or for a very long time)*.

The only way to lose weight permanently is to completely change your attitudes toward food.

Are you sure you want to permanently delete all the items and subfolders?

Polished *[Adjective]* *(clean and shiny as a result of being rubbed, usually with a chemical substance)*.

He polished the table until it gleamed.

He polished his shoes.

LETTER R

Reluctant *[Adjective]* *(unwilling and hesitant to do something because you do not want to do it).*

Tom is reluctant to leave.

She seems reluctant to admit it.

Remind of *[Verb]* *(to make somebody remember something that happened).*

The picture reminds her of her school days.

This house reminds me of my old cottage where I lived 10 years ago.

Reckon *[Verb]* *(to think or have an opinion about something).*

I reckon that you are right.

I reckon that we'll have to leave early.

I reckon it's time to go to the beach.

Removable *[Adjective]* *(easily removed; able to be removed).*

Because it's removable, the cable can be used anywhere.

It's removable and reusable.

Recount *[Verb]* *(to narrate; to tell someone about something that you experienced).*

My uncle sometimes recounted to me stories of his time as a teenager.

My friend recounted to me the tale of his first day at a new job.

Roughly *[Adverb]* *(approximately).*

In the IELTS writing task 2, I wrote roughly 300 words for my essay.

Run into difficulties *[Expression]* *(to experience or get into a difficult situation).*

We've run into difficulties with the new project.

Divorced couples might run into difficulties.

Regret *[Verb] (to feel sorry, disappointed, or remorseful about something that has happened or been done).*

She regretted not having attended the university earlier.

I regret not speaking to him before he left.

Rival *[Noun] (competitor).*

Jack and Jill are rivals in the sportswear business.

The two football clubs are rivals.

To rest *[Verb] (to take a break or relax from some activity).*

We needed to rest after a hard day at work.

We had a short rest after lunch.

Review *[Verb] (to look over, study, or examine again).*

We need to review the case.

I need time to review the situation.

She attended this course to review her Japanese.

Rebellious *[Adjective] (opposing the ideas or rules of authority).*

Her son is a rebellious teenager.

Tom is a rebellious boy.

This student is so rebellious. He never obeys the school rules. If the teacher tells him to wear his school uniform, he turns up in dirty jeans.

Resourcefulness *[Noun] (the ability to be good at finding quick and clever ways to overcome difficulties).*

Her resourcefulness was the main reason he had hired her.

His energy was unbounded, and his resourcefulness overcame every obstacle.

Reinforce *[Verb] (to strengthen; to make something stronger).*

The building is covered by a reinforced concrete roof.

The walls have been reinforced in an attempt to minimize damage in the event of an earthquake.

Repetitive *[Adjective] (doing the same thing over and over again, so that it becomes boring).*

From my point of view, it is a repetitive job. All of the tasks repeat regularly.

Refuge *[Noun] (a place that provides safety or protection).*

A police station is a refuge for people who are in trouble.

My father's greenhouse is his refuge from our noisy home.

To read over *[Verb] (to read something carefully from beginning to end to look for mistakes or to check details).*

Tom carefully read over the contract before he signed it.

I went back and read over the book more thoroughly.

Respiratory disorder *[Noun] (an illness or problems affecting the respiratory system).*

Smoking is particularly dangerous for people who have respiratory disorders.

Pneumonia is a respiratory disorder that causes the sufferer's lungs to become inflamed with.

Realization *[Noun] (the process of achieving or fulfilling an aim, desire or ambition).*

I was shocked by the realization of what I had done.

When he passed the exam, it was the realization of his dream!

Rivalry *[Noun] (the act of competing for the same thing in the same field).*

In Spain, there is a great rivalry between the football teams of Madrid and Barcelona.

Dogs and cats have a notorious history of rivalry.

Reluctance *[Noun] (the feeling of unwillingness to do something (not wanting to do something)).*

His reluctance to answer her questions made her suspicious.

There was evidence of her reluctance to discuss some element of the accident.

LETTER S

Sink in *[Verb] (to become completely understood, known or realized).*

It took a moment for the words to sink in.

Pauses should be used to give time for ideas to sink in.

Sparingly *[Adverb] (in an economical way; in small quantities).*

He knew that his funds were limited so he has spent his money sparingly.

Wearing old clothes and buying scantily of food, Sarah spent her money sparingly.

Sponsor *[Noun] (a person or organization that pays for or contributes to the costs of an event).*

The event was sponsored by several local businesses.

Stuffed bear *[Noun] (a stuffed toy in the shape of a bear).*

A stuffed bear with glasses and a tie.

I gave my daughter an adorable stuffed bear for her birthday.

The shore *[Noun] (the land along the edge of a sea, lake or river).*

I like to walk along the shore.

The shore was littered with rubbish left by the tourists.

Simplify *[Verb] (make something simple/ less complicated and easy to do or understand).*

He tried to simplify your explanation for the children.

She simplified her sentences to use words and phrases she was more comfortable with.

To some degree *[Expression] (to some extent).*

To some degree, he was right.

He can be trusted to some degree.

Sensitivity *[Noun] (the ability to understand the feelings of others).*

She is not known for her sensitivity in dealing with complaints.

Women like him for his sensitivity and charming vulnerability.

Storytelling *[Noun] (the art of telling stories).*

The student has lost the thread of her storytelling.

The teacher has to develop a number of skills to improve her storytelling.

Setback *[Noun] (a difficulty or problem that delays something or makes a situation worse).*

The team suffered a setback when their best player was injured.

Superb *[Adjective] (excellent; very good).*

The diners complimented the chef on the superb meal.

The restaurant has superb food quality, superb service, and superb decor.

To stem from *[Verb] (to be caused by / as the result of something).*

His problems stem from his difficult childhood.

Her headaches stemmed from vision problems.

(To) surround *[Verb] (to be all around someone or something).*

The island is surrounded by fresh water.

She is surrounded by her loving family.

He is surrounded by police officers.

To squander a chance/an opportunity *[Expression] (to waste/fail to use a* *chance, by not taking advantage of it).*

He squandered a chance by not retaking his CPF test, and he totally regretted it.

She squandered a chance to go to university by failing to study for her entrance exam.

Substandard *[Adjective] (below the required standard).*

Substandard housing conditions.

Too many families are still living in substandard housing.

To sift information *[Expression] (to remove unwanted or less useful information).*

As she sifted information, she reached some alarming conclusions.

Our unconscious brain automatically sifts information.

To strike somebody as *[Expression] (to give somebody a particular impression).*

Her reaction struck me as odd.

His appearance struck him as strange.

Self-explanatory *[Adjective] (easy to understand and needs no more explanation).*

This document is self-explanatory.

The email appended below is self-explanatory.

The code sample is self-explanatory and it is very clear how the code works now.

Secure in the knowledge *[Expression] (feeling safe or secure because you know something well).*

The babysitter is available to secure in the knowledge that my kids are safe and sound.

She went on holiday, secure in the knowledge that she had done well in the exam.

Spot *[Noun] (a particular area or place).*

He always sits in the same spot in the library, near the window so that he can look out over the river.

Second to none *[Expression] (as good as or better than all others of the same kind).*

Her cakes are second to none.

The delicious Japanese food in this restaurant is second to none.

Suit someone down to the ground *[Expression] (to be completely suitable, convenient or right for someone).*

America suits him down to the ground.

This new job suits her down to the ground.

To seat *[Verb] (to arrange for someone to sit somewhere).*

The delegates have to be seated according to protocol.

The waiter greeted me with a big smile and seated me by the window.

Souvenir *[Noun] (something you buy or keep as a reminder of a place, an occasion or a holiday/vacation).*

The more my mom looks at her souvenir coffee mug, the more she wants to go back to New York.

I bought a model of a red London bus as a souvenir of my trip to London.

To stand out *[Verb] (to be prominent or more important than somebody/something).*

Her bright dress always makes her stand out in a crowd.

Their old red car stood out from all the rest.

To stem from *[Verb] (to be the result of something).*

The problems stemmed from a power failure at a data center.

Her headaches stemmed from vision problems.

Social isolation *[Noun] (the state of isolating/separating someone from society)*.

It is necessary to apply the form of social isolation towards people who are violent or dangerous to others.

Social isolation is usually connected with increased mortality.

Spread throughout *[Verb] (to open, arrange, or place something over a large area)*.

The fire spread throughout the house.

The news of their marriage spread throughout the village.

Set to *[Verb] (likely to)*.

We are set to meet in Washington on Thursday.

I was happy to know that everything was set to go.

Sustain *[Verb] (support something/somebody physically or mentally in order to be able to continue to live)*.

The ship appeared not to sustain any damage.

In the past, sailors took large supplies of fresh water and food on their ships to sustain them on their long voyages.

Settle *[Verb] (to go and live permanently in a particular place)*.

After her father died, she decided to settle in Sydney.

We are planning to settle in Australia in the near future.

Sex discrimination *[Noun] (the practice of treating somebody or a particular group in society unequally because of their gender)*.

The new sex discrimination law protects men and women from unfair treatment when they are looking for a job.

The law to fight sex discrimination in employment and education.

Subsidise *[Verb] (support an organization financially to help to pay for something)*.

The food is subsidised, so it's much cheaper than elsewhere.

Farming is partly subsidised by the government.

Sustainable *[Adjective] (involving the use of natural products or energy in a way that causes little or no damage to the environment).*

Hydroelectricity is very sustainable.

The ecosystem was sustainable.

Sparingly *[Adverb] (using very little of something in an infrequent manner; in small quantities).*

Because she prefers to have a natural look, she uses cosmetics sparingly.

We should use water sparingly because it is a resource that is essential to sustain life.

Stem from = as the result of = to be caused by

His idea to give roses to his mom for her birthday stems from her love of flowers.

The present crisis in health care stems from the lack of funding by the government.

Sited *[Verb] (to be placed or built in a particular place).*

The castle is sited on a hill near the river, originally to protect the town against enemies.

The drama hall is sited behind the main school building.

Speed up *[Verb] (make something move or travel faster).*

Modernization is the key to speed up our agricultural development.

We'll never get there if he doesn't speed up.

Suited *[Adjective] (right or appropriate for somebody or something).*

Tom and Mary seem to be suited for each other.

This diet is suited to anyone who wants to lose weight.

Serviceable *[Adjective] (suitable to be used; helpful, useful).*

Some of these old tools are still serviceable.

The chairs are old, but still serviceable.

The tyres are worn but still serviceable.

Sound reasons *[Noun] (good and sensible reasons).*

The candidate gave sound reasons for his decision to apply for the job.

There are sound reasons for questioning accuracy and fairness in the application of the death penalty.

Self-interest *[Noun] (considering only the advantage to one's own advantage and well-being, without caring about others).*

She cannot abandon her husband for the sake of self-interest and personal gain.

Self-interest is not only the major driver in human behavior to live a happy life.

Scrupulously *[Adverb] (in a very careful and thorough way, with great care and attention to every detail).*

He is always scrupulously honest in his business activities.

Teachers have to be scrupulously fair in marking examination papers.

Sophisticated *[Adjective] (complicated or complex).*

They're making very sophisticated weapons.

The network connection devices employ very sophisticated programming.

Sweaty *[Adjective] (covered in sweat that makes you feel hot and uncomfortable).*

Tom's palms were sweaty and his mouth was dry.

After working in the garden all day, his clothes were all sweaty, and covered with dirt.

Shrink *[Verb] (become smaller in size or amount).*

The department has been shrinking year by year because of budget cuts.

The Japanese population is shrinking.

Stressed out *[Adverb] (being anxious, worried and nervous).*

She is stressed out about all the work she has at the moment.

I've been really stressed out at work recently.

Sanity *[Noun] (the ability to think and behave in a normal manner without being mentally ill).*

People have begun to doubt her sanity.

He'd been behaving so strangely that they began to doubt his sanity.

To strike up (a conversation, a relationship) *[Expression] (to start (to do) something).*

She was keen to strike up a conversation with him.

She would often strike up conversations with complete strangers.

LETTER T

Thoroughness *[Noun] (the act of doing something very carefully and with great attention to detail).*

I was surprised and impressed with his thoroughness and knowledge of the software.

I admired her understanding and her thoroughness of the psychiatric process.

Throw a party *[Expression] (to hold a party).*

We threw a huge house-warming party last night.

My roommates and I throw parties every weekend.

Treasure *[Verb] (to store or keep (in mind) something that is very special or valuable).*

I shall always treasure the time my family spent together.

I will always treasure the moment when we met.

Thanks to *[Expression] (as a result of/ because of; with the help of).*

Thanks to his help, I passed the exam.

I'll be able to attend college thanks to my parents.

To watch someone's back *[Expression] (to protect someone against danger from an unexpected situation).*

The police officer's partner always watches his back.

I am happy that you watched my back.

Turn down *[Verb] (reject an offer made by someone).*

I turned her invitation down.

The conversation ended when I turned his offer down.

Thought-provoking *[Verb] (making someone think seriously about a particular subject or issue).*

This is an entertaining yet thought-provoking film.

There was a thought-provoking article about poverty in the paper.

(To) take something into account *[Expression] (to consider particular facts before making a decision about something).*

If they took inflation into account, they actually spent less then.

Tom hopes his teacher will take into account the fact that he was ill just before the examination when the teacher evaluates his test paper.

Thanks to (something or someone) *[Expression] (as a result of, owing to, due to, because of (used to express the idea that something is good)).*

Thanks to my help, he passed the exam.

He was found guilty, thanks to the testimony of the witness.

Turn into = become *[Verb] (be transformed into).*

The caterpillar turned into a butterfly.

When she changed to a different school, she turned into a model student.

Turn to *[Verb] (to go in a new direction to improve a situation).*

He turned to teach after working for a company for many years.

To save his regime, Kim turned to the nuclear option.

Take special note of *[Expression] (to pay a special attention to something).*

He took special note of practice in the courts of Florence.

I took special note of their names.

To tell off *[Expression] (to speak or criticize someone angrily because he/she has done* *something wrong).*

She was told off for being careless.

He was told off for being late.

(To) turn out *[Verb] (to be discovered to be something).*

He thought he would get a pay rise, but it turned out to be a false alarm.

The photos he took with his digital camera look good, but when tried to enlarge them, they turned out pretty blurry.

To keep abreast of *[Expression] (to have the most recent and important information about something).*

We must renovate our social life to keep abreast of the times.

It is difficult to keep abreast of the international situation these days.

LETTER U

Unspecified *[Adjective] (not mentioned or stated exactly or clearly).*

I heard a noise at an unspecified point in the night.

At some unspecified time in the past, I went to Italy.

Understandable *[Adjective] (to be easy to understand or comprehend (seems normal and reasonable in a particular situation)).*

His anger is understandable, given what happened.

Being nervous before an operation is really understandable.

Ultimately *[Adverb] (at the end).*

He ultimately decided to go to college.

She ultimately participated in the test to get the certificate.

Unfamiliar *[Adjective] (not familiar, unknown or not recognized).*

We are unfamiliar with the customs of this country.

The landscape is unfamiliar to me.

Unglamorous *[Adjective] (not attractive or exciting).*

Their work is hard and unglamorous, and most people would find it boring.

He worked an unglamorous job in a catering company in Western Sydney.

Unfamiliarity *[Noun] (the fact of lacking knowledge or experience of something; not familiar).*

His temporary shyness was due to his unfamiliarity with the environment.

Her unfamiliarity was not surprising; she had little acquaintance with the stock market.

Unexpected *[Adjective] (surprising; not expected).*

Life is unexpected.

His divorce was totally unexpected.

Unnecessary *[Adjective] (not necessary; needless; unessential).*

Some people feel that holiday insurance is unnecessary.

It is unnecessary to cook for now. I am not hungry.

Unreasonable *[Adjective] (something that is not reasonable; beyond what can be accepted).*

The costs to rent a car in the city are unreasonable.

He was offended by her unreasonable quarrel.

Universal *[Adjective] (involving all people or things in the world).*

Declining health is a universal characteristic of old age.

English is a universal language and is used all over the world.

Unquestionable *[Adjective] (not able to be doubted; obvious and undeniable).*

The sincerity of her beliefs is unquestionable.

His competence as a teacher is unquestionable.

Update = up to date *[Verb] (to make something more modern).*

The company decided to update its computer software.

The most recent weather update said it'll be sunny tomorrow.

Unthinkable *[Adjective] (unimaginable (impossible to imagine or accept)).*

It would be unthinkable to ask him to do that.

In the past, parents allowed their children to play freely in the street, but this is unthinkable nowadays.

Unscrupulous *[Adjective] (dishonest, unfair and without moral principles).*

He runs an unscrupulous business.

The innocent are often deceived by the unscrupulous.

LETTER V

Vast *[Adjective]* *(very big/ extremely large).*

The Sahara is a vast sandy desert.

The Amazon is a vast rainforest.

Vitally important *[Adjective]* *(very important).*

It is vitally important for students to be taught the strategies for using IT.

It is vitally important to keep your teeth clean and healthy.

Viewpoint *[Noun]* *(point of view; opinion).*

They adopted my viewpoint.

His viewpoint is limited.

Various *[Adjective]* *(different, a variety of, many types of).*

This room is used for various purposes.

There are various ways of solving the problem.

There are various kinds of coffee.

Vivid *[Adjective]* *(producing very strong and clear memories in your mind).*

He could remember the dream in vivid detail.

My memories are still vivid.

Venerable *[Adjective]* *(someone or something that deserves respect).*

The cathedral is a venerable building.

Her venerable father died yesterday after a prolonged illness.

Virtually *[Adverb]* *(almost entirely or very nearly).*

It is virtually the same.

The entire town was virtually destroyed.

Versatile *[Adjective]* *(having many different functions and to be used for many different purposes).*

Jeans and T-shirts are versatile and used in both the modern workplace and leisure activities.

It is a versatile industrial material.

Virtually *[Adverb]* *(nearly; almost).*

The entire town was virtually destroyed.

After the discounts, it's virtually free.

Vital *[Adjective]* *(very important, or necessary).*

In fact, sleep is vital to us.

Education is vital to the cultural life of a society.

He played a vital role in winning the game.

LETTER W

Weigh up the pros and cons *[Expression] (to consider/compare carefully the advantages and disadvantages of something before making a decision).*

You must weigh up the pros and cons of changing your job before making your final decision.

He has weighed up the pros and cons of telling me the truth.

Widely perceived *[Expressin] (something that is understood, realized, regarded or thought about in a particular way by a lot of people).*

Science subjects are widely perceived as demanding in terms of both workload and intellectual content.

Working in scientific research is widely perceived as an unglamorous job.

CONCLUSION

Thank you again for downloading this book on *"IELTS Academic Vocabulary: Master 3000+ Academic Vocabularies by Topics Explained in 10 Minutes a Day (3 books in 1 Box set)"* and reading all the way to the end. I'm extremely grateful.

If you know of anyone else who may benefit from the useful list of academic vocabularies that are revealed in this book, please help me inform them of this book. I would greatly appreciate it.

Finally, if you enjoyed this book and feel that it has added value to your work and study in any way, please take a couple of minutes to share your thoughts and post a REVIEW on Amazon. Your feedback will help me to continue to write other books of IELTS topic that helps you get the best results. Furthermore, if you write a simple REVIEW with positive words for this book on Amazon, you can help hundreds or perhaps thousands of other readers who may want to improve their IELTS lexical resource band score. Like you, they worked hard for every penny they spend on books. With the information and recommendation you provide, they would be more likely to take action right away. We really look forward to reading your review.

Thanks again for your support and good luck!

If you enjoy my book, please write a POSITIVE REVIEW on Amazon.

-- Rachel Mitchell --

CHECK OUT OTHER BOOKS

Go here to check out other related books that might interest you:

IELTS Listening Strategies: The Ultimate Guide with Tips, Tricks and Practice on How to Get a Target Band Score of 8.0+ in 10 Minutes a Day.

https://www.amazon.com/dp/B07845S1MG

IELTS Reading Strategies: The Ultimate Guide with Tips and Tricks on How to Get a Target Band Score of 8.0+ in 10 Minutes a Day.

https://www.amazon.com/dp/B077TWDSJJ

Ielts Writing Task 2 Samples : Over 450 High-Quality Model Essays for Your Reference to Gain a High Band Score 8.0+ In 1 Week (Box set) https://www.amazon.com/dp/B077BYQLPG

Ielts Academic Writing Task 1 Samples: Over 450 High Quality Samples for Your Reference to Gain a High Band Score 8.0+ In 1 Week (Box set) https://www.amazon.com/dp/B077CC5ZG4

**Shortcut To English Collocations: Master 2000+ English Collocations
In Used Explained Under 20 Minutes A Day (5 books in 1 Box set)**

https://www.amazon.com/dp/B06W2P6S22

IELTS Writing Task 1 + 2: The Ultimate Guide with Practice to Get a Target Band Score of 8.0+ In 10 Minutes a Day

https://www.amazon.com/dp/B075DFYPG6

IELTS Speaking Strategies: The Ultimate Guide With Tips, Tricks, And Practice On How To Get A Target Band Score Of 8.0+ In 10 Minutes A Day.

https://www.amazon.com/dp/B075JCW65G

Shortcut To Ielts Writing: The Ultimate Guide To Immediately Increase Your Ielts Writing Scores.

https://www.amazon.com/dp/B01JV7EQGG

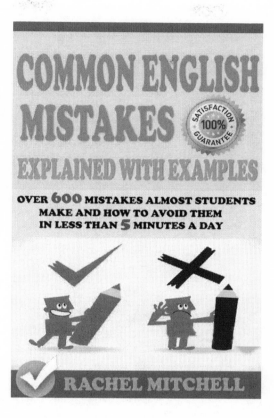

Common English Mistakes Explained With Examples: Over 600
Mistakes Almost Students Make and How to Avoid Them in Less
Than 5 Minutes A Day

https://www.amazon.com/dp/B072PXVHNZ

Paraphrasing Strategies: 10 Simple Techniques For Effective
Paraphrasing In 5 Minutes Or Less

https://www.amazon.com/dp/B071DFG27Q

Legal Vocabulary In Use: Master 600+ Essential Legal Terms And Phrases Explained In 10 Minutes A Day

http://www.amazon.com/dp/B01L0FKXPU

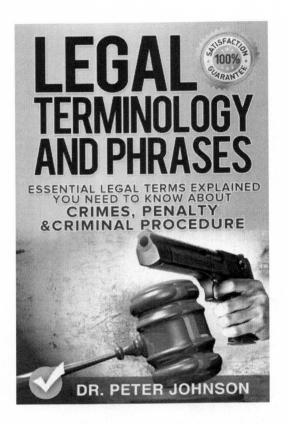

Legal Terminology And Phrases: Essential Legal Terms Explained
You Need To Know About Crimes, Penalty And Criminal Procedure

http://www.amazon.com/dp/B01L5EB54Y

Productivity Secrets For Students: The Ultimate Guide To Improve
Your Mental Concentration, Kill Procrastination, Boost Memory And
Maximize Productivity In Study

http://www.amazon.com/dp/B01JS52UT6

Daughter of Strife: 7 Techniques On How To Win Back Your
Stubborn Teenage Daughter

https://www.amazon.com/dp/B01HS5E3V6

Parenting Teens With Love And Logic: A Survival Guide To Overcoming The Barriers Of Adolescence About Dating, Sex And Substance Abuse

https://www.amazon.com/dp/B01JQUTNPM

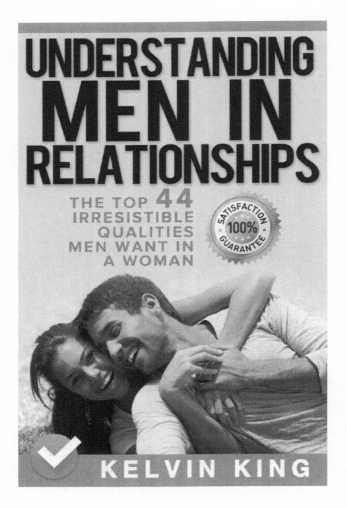

http://www.amazon.com/dp/B01K0ARNA4

Made in the USA
Las Vegas, NV
13 December 2023

82684756R00192